THE FIRST AGE OF CHRISTIANITY

THE FIRST AGE OF CHRISTIANITY

By
ERNEST F. SCOTT, D. D.
*Professor of Biblical Theology in Union Theological Seminary
New York*

WIPF & STOCK · Eugene, Oregon

Wipf and Stock Publishers
199 W 8th Ave, Suite 3
Eugene, OR 97401

The First Age of Christianity
By Scott, Ernest F.
Softcover ISBN-13: 978-1-6667-5611-1
Hardcover ISBN-13: 978-1-6667-5612-8
eBook ISBN-13: 978-1-6667-5613-5
Publication date 8/12/2022
Previously published by George Allen & Unwin, 1925

This edition is a scanned facsimile of the original edition published in 1925.

PREFACE

The study of the New Testament has now become highly specialized, and the results of the modern investigation are scattered through a great number of works, most of them written for professional scholars. There seems to be room for a book which will present in brief compass and readable form the main conclusions. It is impossible in the space available to do more than indicate the many difficult problems, each of which would require a volume to itself; but something may be gained by the endeavor to present the early Christian movement as a living whole. New Testament history and literature and theology are so often treated as separate subjects that we are in danger of forgetting that they are bound up together, and cannot be rightly understood except in their mutual relation. Without a map of the whole country little can be made of the various sections.

The book is intended primarily as introductory to the study of Christian origins from the modern point of view. A hope may be expressed that it may also be of service to more advanced scholars who wish to collect and harmonize their knowledge.

E. F. SCOTT.

New York,
Nov. 6th, 1925.

CONTENTS

CHAPTER   **PAGE**

I. THE HISTORICAL BACKGROUND

   (1) THE PEOPLE OF ISRAEL 11
   (2) PALESTINE IN THE TIME OF CHRIST 23
   (3) THE ROMAN EMPIRE 31

II. THE GOSPEL RECORD 45

III. THE LIFE OF JESUS

   (1) THE EARLIER LIFE 58
   (2) THE MINISTRY 66
   (3) THE PASSION 76

IV. THE TEACHING OF JESUS

   (1) THE RELIGIOUS BASIS 89
   (2) THE ETHICAL TEACHING 98
   (3) THE MESSIANIC CLAIM 102

V. THE PRIMITIVE CHURCH

   (1) THE SOURCES 108
   (3) THE CONVERSION OF PAUL 113
   (4) THE COUNCIL OF JERUSALEM 123
   (5) THE GREAT MISSION 126
   (6) THE CAPTIVITY AND DEATH OF PAUL 132
   (7) THE CHURCH AFTER PAUL 148
   (2) THE BEGINNING OF THE CHURCH 158

CONTENTS

CHAPTER PAGE

VI. THE DEVELOPMENT OF NEW TESTAMENT THOUGHT
- (1) THE NATURE OF THE DEVELOPMENT 175
- (2) PRIMITIVE CHRISTIANITY 179
- (3) THE THEOLOGY OF PAUL 188
- (4) THE PAULINE SCHOOL 207
- (5) THE ALEXANDRIAN INFLUENCE 210
- (6) THE EPISTLE TO THE HEBREWS 213
- (7) THE GOSPEL AND EPISTLES OF JOHN 217
- (8) POPULAR CHRISTIANITY 228

THE FIRST AGE OF CHRISTIANITY

CHAPTER I

THE HISTORICAL BACKGROUND

(1) THE PEOPLE OF ISRAEL

Palestine, the cradle of our religion, is a strip of mountainous country on the eastern edge of the Mediterranean sea. It measures one hundred and fifty miles from north to south, while its breadth varies from twenty-five to about eighty miles. This little territory, however, is the gateway of three continents, and from the earliest times has been exposed to the shock of war. Its people lived continually under the shadow of danger, and out of their bitter experiences grew the religion which they gave to the world.

About 1400 or 1300 B.C., Palestine was occupied by the wandering tribes who finally became the nation of Israel. At that time the Egyptian and Hittite and Babylonian empires had worn themselves down by mutual warfare, and the conquering Assyrian power had not yet arisen. There was an interval of some centuries in which a small nation was free to develop an independent life, and to this period belongs the history which is recorded in the Old Testament. From the beginning the Hebrews were a virile and highly gifted race, with a profound feeling for religion. They had brought with them out of the desert a few simple beliefs, and a law of worship and conduct associated with the great name of Moses. During the centuries of settled life this primitive religion was developed in many directions, and at the same time was mingled with superstitious elements from the native Palestinian cults. It was not till the age of the great prophets, in the eighth century B.C., that the higher conceptions, latent from the first in the religion of Israel, were disentangled, and became fully operative. The prophets declared, in language of matchless force and beauty, that the God worshipped in Israel was the one true God, who would at last be acknowledged by the whole world. He was above all a God of righteousness, who governed men and nations by eternal moral laws. The service He required did not consist in prayers and ceremonies, but in justice, mercy, humility, care for the poor and oppressed, purity, and uprightness. It must not be supposed that the nation as a whole responded to the lofty teaching of the prophets. Religion for the majority was still a matter of festivals and sacrifices and traditional customs. It had its centre in the temple of Jerusalem, where an army of priests, holding office by hereditary right, performed the stated ordinances. But the prophetic teaching left a deep impression. In the course of time it leavened and transformed the old ceremonial religion, and the change was hastened by the calamities which were now overtaking the nation.

Under three strong kings, Saul, David, and Solomon, a united people had formed itself out of the scattered tribes, and bade fair, at one time, to dominate the whole of Syria. But there had always been a cleavage, which gave rise, after the wasteful reign of Solomon, to open division. Instead of combining its forces to meet the dangers which were already looming on the horizon, Israel broke into two small kingdoms which were always at strife with one another. They both found themselves helpless when the conquering march of Assyria had at last begun. Samaria, the northern kingdom and by far the larger and stronger, was destroyed in 721 B.C., and the people were transported to the region of the Euphrates, where they were absorbed into the population of the east. The nation was now reduced to the tiny southern kingdom of Judah, which contrived by careful policy to maintain itself for another century. The respite was all-important, for it was this age which saw the culmination of the great prophetic movement in Isaiah, Jeremiah and the unknown author of Deuteronomy. Through these men and others like them the primitive beliefs of the Hebrew people gave birth to the highest spiritual religion which the world had yet known.

With the fall of Niniveh (608–7 B.C.) the Assyrian menace was removed, and Judah, along with the small neighbouring kingdoms, ventured to assert its freedom. But it was now thrown into conflict with the rising power of Babylon, and after some years of suspense Jerusalem was taken and demolished in 586 B.C. The people were carried captive to Babylon, but the national consciousness had now been deepened by the work of the prophets, and they held firmly together. Fifty years afterwards, when Cyrus, the enlightened Persian conqueror, had put an end to the Babylonian empire and offered liberty to the oppressed races, a large body of Judaeans returned to their own country. Jerusalem was slowly re-built and a new temple took the place of that which had been destroyed. Recovery was difficult after the great disaster, and for a long time the population was small and poverty-stricken. It was shielded, however, from external danger by the powerful Persian monarchy in which it was now incorporated, and in two centuries of peace the little community gradually extended itself. One province, that of Samaria, had been given by the Assyrians to a number of alien tribes who continued to hold possession, but the rest of Palestine was inhabited again, as in the time of David, by people of the Hebrew race.

It was in the period after the exile that the religion of Israel began to assume a new character. The ancient customs were now codified in the Law, which was made binding on all men and women of Hebrew descent. At the same time the temple assumed a place which it had not hitherto occupied in the life of the people. All religious observance was centralized in the temple, and the high aspirations which came to cluster around it found expression in the Psalms, which grew out of its worship. This ritual religion was saved from mere formalism by those prophetic convic-

FIRST AGE OF CHRISTIANITY 15

tions which had now rooted themselves in the general mind. The Law, while it perpetuated much that belonged to a bygone age, had allied itself with the ideas of the prophets. Without its aid they could hardly have become effective in the ordinary religion.

Palestine, with the rest of the Persian empire, submitted to Alexander the Great after his marvellous series of victories. On his death in 323 B.C. his conquests were divided among his chief lieutenants, and Palestine for a time was attached to the new kingdom of Egypt. Eventually it fell to Syria, which was governed by a line of Macedonian kings who usually bore the name of Antiochus. It does not appear that the people troubled themselves much with those political changes. They were subject, whatever happened, to foreign masters, and so long as they were left free to observe their own customs they accepted the government in power. In course of time they would have been fused in the general life of the Syrian kingdom, and perhaps would have lost all traces of a peculiar nationality. There was a singular fascination in the Greek culture which had been planted in the East by the Macedonian conquerors. Intelligent men could not but perceive the vast superiority of Greek art and thought and literature, while the Greek modes of living had a brightness and charm which appealed to every one. Even Greek religion, with its lovely myths and festivals, its glorious expression in sculpture and architecture, made a strong impression on the popular mind. Within a century after Alexander's death the Jews were the only Eastern people who had not yielded to the Greek influence, and they too were on the point of submission. But in 168 B.C. the Syrian king, Antiochus Epiphanes, impatient with the slow progress of the assimilation, determined to hasten it by force. Jewish customs like circumcision and the observance of the Sabbath were proscribed under severe penalties. Altars and statues to the Greek divinities were set up, even in the precincts of the temple. The effect of all this, as might have been foreseen, was to drive the people into rebellion. For ten years, under the leadership of the heroic priestly family of the Maccabees, they made war with varying fortunes on their oppressors, and at last succeeded in winning their independence. Again, after four hundred years, there was a Jewish kingdom, at the head of which now stood the Maccabean, or Asmonaean, house, which had led the movement for liberty. In virtue of his priestly descent the Asmonaean king could also hold the office of high-priest thus recalling the legendary Melchizedek, who was at once king and priest in Jerusalem.[1]

The Maccabean revolt was of the utmost consequence for the religion as well as for the outward fortunes of the Jewish people. (1) From this time onward the temple became quite subordinate to the Law. It was the customs of the Law which had been attacked by the heathen power and had been victoriously maintained. The victory, too,

---
[1] Gen. xiv. 18. cf. Ps. cx.

FIRST AGE OF CHRISTIANITY 17

had been achieved by a great popular effort, while the higher priesthood for the most part had stood aloof or had sided with the invaders. It was natural that the piety and patriotism of the common people should find their centre in the Law. The temple henceforth was little more than a survival, honoured because its services were necessary to the due fulfilment of the Law. The scribes who transmitted and expounded the Law had no official position, but they and not the priests were the real leaders of the nation. (2) New beliefs were now adopted into the Jewish religion and largely changed its character. It always happens that in a period of supreme crisis men are thrown back on ultimate questions which perhaps have troubled them little in more peaceful times. Such questions presented themselves in an acute form during the Maccabean struggle. Why had the righteous God exposed His people to suffering, and apparently deserted His own cause? What was the purpose He was working towards in his dealing with the world? What had become of the men and women who in their devotion to Him had suffered martyrdom? In Old Testament religion the question of personal immortality had scarcely arisen. Even the prophets had been content to believe in the permanence of the nation, which God would safeguard whatever became of its individual members. This belief could no longer satisfy. It was felt that if God was just He must reward His faithful servants. Not only did this hope for personal immortality now arise, but the ancient idea of the permanence of the nation itself underwent a change. It was believed that a new age was coming in which God would exalt His people Israel. The present order would come to an end and an angelic being, the Messiah, would descend from heaven to judge the world and make all things new. The righteous of past times would be raised up and would be united with the living in a holy community which would inherit the new age. These ideas of the future had sprung from the Old Testament, but their development was fostered by the Persian influence which had acted powerfully on Jewish thought since the return from exile. The old Persian religion, based on the teachings of Zoroaster, may be ranked next to that of Israel itself as the purest and most elevated of all ancient forms of worship. It rested on the belief that two principles are in eternal conflict—Light and Darkness, Good and Evil, Ahura Mazda and Ahriman. Man is called to take his part in this great warfare, and according as he acquits himself will be his destiny. Persian religion thus concerned itself largely with speculations about the future. It looked forward to a new age and a Redeemer who would bring it in. It taught the doctrine of immortality, and of rewards and punishments in the other world. These conceptions were interwoven with a mythology, often grotesque but sometimes impressive and beautiful, which in large measure was taken over by Jewish thinkers in their efforts to spell out the mysteries of the future. A spirit of speculation, hitherto foreign to Hebrew thought,

FIRST AGE OF CHRISTIANITY 19

thus found its way into the later Judaism. It was called forth by the calamities of the time, and availed itself of doctrines and imaginations borrowed from Persia. This interest in the future and the secrets of the unseen world gave birth to a new type of literature which was eagerly cultivated during the next two centuries, and which is known as Apocalyptic. Usually it takes the form of visions supposed to have been vouchsafed to Enoch, Moses, Baruch, Ezra or some other great figure of the past. The earliest, and in many respects the most important of those apocalyptic writings, was incorporated in the Old Testament as the Book of Daniel. Within the last century a large number of similar books, most of which had been completely lost, have been recovered, and have thrown a flood of light on the ideas which underlie the New Testament teaching.

The period of Jewish independence may be reckoned at just one hundred years (164–64 B.C.). The new kingdom had begun under the brightest auspices. Able and patriotic kings were at the head of a nation elated by its high achievements in the war of freedom, and confident of the future. In the apocalyptic literature of that time the hope is entertained that the existing prosperity will continue and grow until it merges in the perfect blessedness of the Kingdom of God. But this mood of hopefulness soon passed away. There had always been a conflict between the two ideals of making Israel a strong political power and of sacrificing everything else to its higher calling as the people of God. During the great patriotic struggle the two ideals went hand in hand, but when the safety of the nation was once assured the old differences reasserted themselves, and became ever more acute. The rising party of the Pharisees denounced the secular government, and declared that God alone was King of Israel. They bitterly felt that the national victory to which they had largely contributed had been turned to mere worldly purposes. Their antagonism more than once led to massacre and civil war.

While it was thus weakening itself by internal strife the little kingdom was threatened by a new danger. Rome had emerged victorious from its long duel with Carthage, and was now building up its empire. From the West it had turned to the East, and in 65 B.C. the famous general Pompey had overcome the last serious resistance offered by the Eastern powers. Just at that time two Asmonaean princes were disputing the succession to the throne, and Pompey was called in to adjudicate their claims. The Jews themselves thus supplied a pretext for the interference of Rome, and in 64 B.C. Pompey took Jerusalem. From this time onward Palestine was absorbed into the Roman system as a subdivision of the great province of Syria.

Shortly after this time the long conflict began which ended in the establishment of the Roman empire under Augustus and his successors. These civil wars were mainly fought out in the East, first between Caesar and Pompey, then between

FIRST AGE OF CHRISTIANITY 21

Brutus and Cassius on the one hand and Antony and Octavian on the other, and finally between Antony and his former colleague. The position of Palestine during the whole of this long period was a critical one, and the comparative security which it enjoyed was due to the skilful policy of the man who was afterwards known as Herod the Great. He was an Idumaean—sprung, that is, from the race of Edom which from the earliest times had been the bitter enemy of Israel. His father Antipater, however, had attained to high rank in the Jewish kingdom during the latter years of the Asmonaean dynasty, and had contrived, by aiding the designs of the Romans, to make himself virtual ruler of the country. After his death, his son Herod had continued his policy of friendship with Rome, and had always the shrewdness to forecast, during the turmoil of the civil wars, which side was likely to prove successful. Again and again he changed his allegiance, and each victor in turn found him a valuable ally, and rewarded him with larger powers. When Octavian finally become sole master of the Roman world and assumed the title of Augustus, he appointed Herod king of Palestine. The country was still tributary to Rome, and Herod was too wise a man ever to aim at an independence which would have brought him no advantage and which could not have been maintained. But with the one proviso that he should govern under Rome and with a view to Roman interests, he reigned as king.

The position of Herod during his long reign

(37–4 B.C.) was an extremely difficult one. On the one hand he was required to satisfy his Roman masters, and on the other to conciliate a people which hated him as a usurper and as the willing instrument of the ruthless heathen power. In order to give his rule some show of legitimacy he allied himself by marriage with the Asmonaean house. His sons by this marriage had a better title than he, and he was led to suspect, perhaps justly, that they were conspiring to displace him. With a temper that was naturally jealous and tyrannical he was well aware that he was surrounded by enemies, and was constantly seeking to consolidate his power by bloodshed. The whole course of his reign was marked by savage outbreaks which culminated in the murder of his own wife and children. His name has become a by-word for all that is most repulsive in Oriental despotism.

None the less there can be no question that he was a great ruler, entitled to the gratitude of the nation that so bitterly hated him. He restrained it from political adventure would could only have plunged it into utter ruin, and raised it by his farsighted administration to a high level of prosperity. He was a tireless builder and a large number of necessary public works were carried out under his direction. In the latter part of his reign he commenced the re-building of the temple, transforming it into one of the most splendid edifices in the world. For a century past the Jews had been widely scattered, and their colonies were to be found in all the great cities of the empire.

FIRST AGE OF CHRISTIANITY 23

Herod made it his aim to improve the standing of those Jews of the Dispersion. By magnificent gifts to one foreign city and another he created the impression that the Jews were a great people, under a wealthy and generous king.

(2) PALESTINE IN THE TIME OF CHRIST

Herod died, after a reign of thirty-three years, in 4 B.C. and his kingdom, by his own bequest, was divided among his three surviving sons. Archelaus ruled in Jerusalem over Judea; Antipas held the middle portion of the country, including Galilee; while the northern and northeastern region went to Philip. None of the sons inherited the father's ability and force of character. Archelaus, indeed, to whom the most difficult task had fallen, proved wholly incompetent, and after nine years his subjects petitioned the emperor that he should be removed. Judea was again attached to the province of Syria, but in view of its peculiar circumstances was placed under a special magistrate—a procurator sent out from Rome. Antipas and Philip continued to administer their tiny kingdoms. Of Philip we know little, but he seems to have been a just and capable ruler, by far the best of the Herodian princes. Antipas was to become memorable as the king of Galilee during the lifetime of Jesus. He comes before us in the Gospels as weak and dissolute and treacherous; and this judgment is confirmed by all that we know of him from other sources. On a narrower stage he displayed all his father's vices, without any of the strong qualities which had partially redeemed them.

At the time, then, when the Gospel history begins Palestine was held firmly within the grasp of the Roman power, although the regions north of Judaea were allowed a shadow of independence under native princes. A century had passed since Rome had entered into possession, but the people had never reconciled themselves to the foreign rule. Several times there had been futile attempts at rebellion, of which the most serious was in 6 A.D., when one Judas stirred up a guerrilla war in Galilee, which was mercilessly put down. For the time being the country was quiet, but there never ceased to be murmurings under the surface. The discontent was already fermenting which was to boil over, forty years later, in the great revolt. It is somewhat difficult to account for this aversion which was felt from the very outset to the Roman supremacy. Palestine, like all the provinces of the empire, was governed justly though sternly, and perhaps there had never been a period in its long history when conditions were so peaceful and life and property so safe. In some respects the government was remarkably tolerant. Aware of the devotion of the people to their religion and ancestral customs the Romans had tried as far as possible to preserve existing institutions. Matters of ordinary administration were left to the local synagogues and the council which met at Jerusalem under the presidency of the high-priest. Perhaps we must explain the Jewish attitude by an

FIRST AGE OF CHRISTIANITY 25

antipathy of temper which made the Jews and the Romans natural enemies. The people had been content with their subject status under the Persians, and had only rebelled against the Syrian kings after wanton provocation. But the hard, matter-of-fact Roman mind could never put itself in sympathy with Jewish sentiment. Again and again when it was most anxious to be just and conciliatory, it offended some scruple or cherished practice which it could only regard as utterly unreasonable. The revolt in Galilee, for example, was due to the taking of a census, which had shocked the religious feeling of the Jews, while for the Romans it was the necessary basis for right administration. Rome failed, as the West has so often done in its effort to govern Eastern peoples, not so much through any grave error as by a want of tact and consideration.

Within the Roman system the Jews maintained their own national life, of which the dominating factor was now the Law. Not only all religious practice but matters of business, domestic relations, jurisprudence, manners and behaviour were regulated by the Law of Moses. Like the Koran among Mohammedan peoples to-day it was at once a Bible, a textbook of all knowledge, and a legal code. Since it was so necessary that all Jews should be well acquainted with the Law an institution had grown up which was destined to be one of the most fruitful that Judaism has bequeathed to the world. Every town and village in the land had now its synagogue, in which the whole life of the community centred. The synagogue, in its primary intention, was not so much a place of worship as a place of instruction. From Sabbath to Sabbath the people met together and the Law was read to them, section by section, so that all might grow familiar with its precepts. The work of expounding it was the office of the scribes. Originally, as their name implies, they had only copied out the sacred text, but in this manner they had acquired a special knowledge of its provisions. It had been designed for a primitive phase of culture, and could not be carried out, just as it was, in a complex society. Many of its crudities had to be softened, and its morality broadened and deepened, before it could be imposed on a fully civilized nation. The scribes undertook this necessary task of developing and qualifying the Law, and their interpretation, when it had been generally accepted, was held to be just as binding as the text itself. This "tradition," however, to distinguish it from the written Law, had to be transmitted by word of mouth and stored in the memory. Accumulating for generations it finally became so vast in extent that no memory could retain it, and it was committed to writing in the collection known as the "Talmud." This did not take place until long after the time of Christ.

It was on the question of the oral tradition that the two great Jewish parties, the Pharisees and the Sadducees, most conspicuously differed. The history of both the parties is obscure, but there is reason to believe that the Pharisees had their origin in a society which was formed shortly before the Maccabaean war for the stricter observance of the Law. Their name appears to mean "the Separated," and the members of the party always held aloof from "the people of the land," the ordinary men and women who could not scrupulously conform to all the legal requirements. The Pharisees took over the "tradition" along with the Law itself, and were thus committed to a task which left them little time for anything else. They were always a small body, numbering about four thousand in the time of Christ, and were chiefly drawn from the more leisured class. But the influence they exercised was out of all proportion to their numbers, and was all the greater because it did not depend on any official status. They claimed to be in reality what all Jews were supposed to be. Israel was the people of the Law, and the Pharisees, who alone were faithful to this ideal vocation, were revered on all sides by their countrymen. Their example set the standard for all right conduct; their judgment on all religious matters was undisputed.

The Sadducees, unlike the Pharisees, were an hereditary caste, consisting of the higher priesthood and their retainers. Their name appears to have been derived from Zadok, who was highpriest in the time of Solomon, and from whom they traced their descent. The Romans, who always ruled as far as possible through the native authorities, had fixed on this priestly aristocracy as the natural leaders of the Jewish people, and had entrusted large powers to their hands. Not only did they provide the high-priest, who was now the chief personage in the nation, but the Sanhedrin, or Great Council, was chiefly composed of Sadducees. In view of the official dignity which they enjoyed they were strongly on the side of the existing order, and were nervously afraid of anything that might lead to revolution. It was this that was to determine their attitude toward the work of Jesus. Between Pharisees and Sadducees there was strong opposition, for on the matter of the Law the Sadducees were conservative. They took their stand on the written word alone, rejecting the tradition. For this reason, and not in any sceptical temper, they denied such doctrines as those of the future life and the existence of a world of spirits. From our reading of the New Testament we are wont to think of the Pharisees as a group of bigots and reactionaries, but the truth is that they represented the progressive movement in Judaism. They admitted new opinions and beliefs, and recognised that the ancient Law if it was still to serve as a rule of practice, must be adapted to new conditions.

The Law, it must always be remembered, was mainly concerned with the outward, ceremonial side of the religious life. It prescribed what a man might eat and drink, how he should perform the stated rites, what his behavior should be in all conceivable circumstances. With matters of opinion it interfered very little. It made no attempt, as the church was to do in later days, to impose a sys-

FIRST AGE OF CHRISTIANITY 29

tem of doctrines which should be binding on all. We have thus the singular phenomenon of a religion which was extremely rigid, and yet allowed the widest latitude in the sphere of belief. A great number of sects and parties flourished within Judaism, and the right of none of them was called in question. One of the most remarkable was the sect of the Essenes, a monastic brotherhood which made its home beyond the Jordan. In some of its teachings it was more closely allied with Persian than with Jewish religion, but since it was scrupulous in the observance of the Law it was regarded not only as orthodox but as exceptionally pious. The latitude in doctrine was especially marked among the Jews of the Dispersion. In their foreign environment they could not but be affected by the modes of thought which were prevalent in the Gentile world. Most of all in the great intellectual centre of Alexandria Jewish thinkers were active in speculation, and interpreted the Law in the light of a mystical theology. None the less they considered themselves faithful Jews. They kept the Sabbath and practised circumcision and observed the distinction between clean and unclean meats. From the point of view of the Law they were irreproachable.

In the time of Christ, therefore, Palestine was a district within the all-embracing Roman Empire. It resented the foreign yoke, but probably at no previous time were the conditions of life so favourable for the great mass of the people. Outside of the few large towns the chief employments were agriculture, sheep-farming and the ordinary handicrafts. We can gather, from the vivid pictures offered us in the Gospels, that life in that rugged country was usually a hard struggle, but the very poverty of the land saved it from some of the worst evils which were elsewhere rampant at that time. Rich merchants and landowners occasionally possessed slaves, but in the small towns and country districts work was entirely done by free laborers. The festivals were few and simple, devoted to religious observance and the natural merry-making at the end of harvest and vintage. There was little leisure for those frequent holidays which gave occasion, in Pagan lands, to vicious self-indulgence. It cannot be questioned, indeed, that morality was on a higher level in Palestine than anywhere else in the empire, and this was mainly due to the discipline of the Law. With all its shortcomings it rested on the moral code summed up in the Ten Commandments. Even its more meaningless requirements were a continual training in habits of self-control and self-examination. The Law, too, which was obligatory on all, established a community of feeling which did not exist elsewhere. Every Jewish man and woman had place in a fellowship bound together by religious ties, and was trained in a sense of social duty. Too often we think only of the protest which Christianity offered to the Law, but we ought also to remember that Christianity grew up in the soil of the Law, and derived from it some of its most precious elements.

FIRST AGE OF CHRISTIANITY 31

(3) THE ROMAN EMPIRE

Palestine occupied a place apart in the great empire in which it was now incorporated. Other nations had become reconciled to the dominion of Rome, and for the most part submitted to it gratefully, as the one means of deliverance from incessant war and confusion. They were in full sympathy, too, with the Pagan ideals on which the Roman power was based, and were easily fused in a common type of civilization. The Jews, faithful to their ancestral Law, could not but feel themselves a peculiar people. Roman officials and soldiers were at once aware when they settled in Palestine that they had passed into a little separate world. None the less this isolated people was now involved, whether it would or not, in the vast empire. Of this they were constantly reminded by the money they used, the presence of foreign troops and magistrates, and the alien language in which all public business was transacted. Every village had sent out emigrants to Greece or Egypt or Italy, and had thus formed links with the wider world.

The world at this time meant the Roman Empire. It was dimly known that there were nations beyond the frontiers, and venturous merchants brought silk and spices from China and India, and amber from the Baltic sea. But for all ordinary purposes the empire was self-contained. Augustus had laid down the rule that its borders were not to be extended, and this rule was observed by his successors. On the west and east it was bounded by the Atlantic Ocean and the river Euphrates; on the north by the Rhine and the Danube; on the south by the Sahara Desert. All the enormous region between, peopled by nearly a hundred separate races, was now under the supreme direction of one man. The forms of the old Republican government were still observed, but while this concession was made to Roman sentiment the empire was an absolute monarchy in all but name. More than a generation had passed since the close of the civil wars, and for all this time there had been almost unbroken peace. During the long reign of Augustus, perhaps the greatest ruler that the world has known, a wonderful system of administration had been perfected, and had secured order and justice for every province. Countries formerly in perpetual turmoil were now busied with commerce and agriculture, and were dotted over with wealthy cities. A network of roads covered the whole empire, and brought the provinces into close intercourse with one another and with Rome, the capital, which was now a city of about two million people and by far the greatest metropolis that had ever been or was to be again for eighteen centuries. Rome was the model which all other cities and even the smaller towns tried to imitate. They reproduced in miniature the plan of the city, the municipal arrangements, the public buildings, the social habits and amusements. As Rome had brought the nations

FIRST AGE OF CHRISTIANITY 33

into one political system, so it imposed on them its own civilization.

In this assimilating process the Greek genius worked hand in hand with the Roman. From the time of their first intercourse with Greece the Romans had acknowledged the superiority of the Greek culture. They were conscious, as Virgil proudly declares, that Rome had the political gift —"to rule the peoples by her power, to establish an order of peace, to spare the vanquished and beat down the proud."[2] But art and literature and philosophy, as the poet admits, were the peculiar birthright of Greece. All educated Romans were familiar with the Greek language and were imbued with Greek ideas. They gladly availed themselves of the attractive power of the Greek genius to unite the races which had come under their dominion. As a result of Alexander's conquests the eastern countries were already permeated with Greek culture, and it now spread to the West. Wherever the Roman peace was enforced there were schools in which the Greek poets and philosophers were studied. All the diverse nations had acquired common standards of life and thought.

The process of fusion did not stop with this adoption of a uniform culture. As the nations came within the same political system they were brought into social and commercial intercourse. Gauls and Spaniards found their way to Italian cities, and in course of time were hardly to be distinguished from the native population. Most re-

[2] *Aeneid* VI, 851.

markable of all and most fruitful of result was the pouring of Eastern blood into the West. Commerce was largely in the hands of Orientals; the Roman army was recruited, in great measure, from the warlike races of Asia Minor; through the slave market the influx of Orientals was so great that it affected the racial qualities of the Mediterranean peoples. All the great cities of the empire were cosmopolitan. In their mingling of languages and nationalities, they were much like the composite American cities of to-day.

That first century is forever memorable as the age which witnessed the birth and early progress of Christianity; but on other grounds it stands out as one of the crowning periods of the world's history. Its significance lies in this—that it marks the culminating phase of the whole life of antiquity. For something like four thousand years men had been advancing, out of the primitive barbarism, towards an ever higher condition. Babylon and Egypt, the various lands of Syria and Asia Minor, finally Greece and Italy, had evolved their different types of civilization. In the Roman empire of the first century these had all converged and mingled. The age-long growth of the life of humanity in that ancient world had attained its flower. Except in the fields of government and practical enterprise the period was not a creative one. It cannot show the name of a single great poet or artist or thinker, although at no previous time had art and literature and philosophy been so eagerly and generally cultivated. Its task was not so much to produce, as

FIRST AGE OF CHRISTIANITY 35

to gather up and blend together all that the previous ages had contributed. The preliminary work was finished. The plans had been drawn and the materials hewn into shape and assembled; and the first century set itself to rear the building—the definite embodiment of the Pagan conception of life. That age, more than any other known to us in history, leaves on us the impression of harmony and attainment. All aims that lay within the horizon of Pagan thought had now been achieved. Conflict had ended, for the Roman peace imposed on all nations seemed destined to endure forever. No further perfection in any art, as its principles were understood by the ancient mind, was now possible. The feeling was everywhere present that all was accomplished, and that nothing was left but to maintain and enjoy the splendid civilization which was now complete.

Such periods of full equilibrium never last long in this unstable world, and the Roman peace was soon to be rudely shaken by internal strife and the incursions of the outside races, and above all by the new ferment which entered through Christianity. When we look more closely into underlying conditions even in the first century we can see that the consummation was at the same time the beginning of a decay. For one thing, the empire, while it had brought the great boon of peace to a divided world, had by that very act crushed out the hope and aspiration necessary to the higher life. Men had formerly lived for their city or tribe. Out of this exalted patriotism had grown the marvellous achievements of the Greek states, of Israel, of Rome itself. The imperial government, with its machine-like efficiency, had made civic sentiment a thing of the past. The old careers and ambitions were now closed, and men's interests grew always narrower. Nothing impresses us more, as we study the records of that time, than the prevailing apathy. Among the higher classes suicide was almost the normal form of death, and it frequently had no other motive than a sense of intolerable weariness. The poor had their daily toil to engross them, but were miserably conscious that they were mere units in a huge multitude in which their individuality meant nothing. One of the features of the time was the growth of societies—workmen's guilds, burial clubs, and religious associations. In his membership of such a group the poor man sought an escape from the monotony of his life. He could feel for an hour, as he took his place in this little circle, that he was a human being, in whom a few fellow creatures had some interest. The Christian church was to prove the greatest and most beneficent of these societies, and here we have one of the prime causes of its amazing progress.

Again, with all its apparent stability, the empire rested on a basis that was radically unsound. In the ancient world slavery was the substitute not only for free labour but for machinery; and Rome, with its vast undertakings, had been forced to develop the slave system to an enormous extent. Great contractors are known to have employed thousands of slaves. Land was cultivated by gangs of slaves, in place of the small farmers who had once been the strength of Italy. So numerous had the slaves become that they were forbidden to wear any distinctive dress or badge which might make them aware of their multitude. The cruelty of the slave system was largely mitigated in the first century by the more humane sentiment of the age. Public opinion now demanded that a good slave, after twenty years of faithful service, should receive his freedom. Facilities were allowed to the slaves to earn and save little sums of money, so that they might buy their liberty even sooner. Great numbers, if not the majority, of slaves eventually became free, and the large class of freedmen served to bridge the gulf between liberty and bondage. But with all its ameliorations the lot of the slave was a bitter one, and the system bore almost more cruelly on the poorer freeman than on the slaves themselves. The artisan who had to work with his own hands had little chance of a livelihood when he had to compete with the great slave owners. Not only so, but many of the most honorable and useful forms of labor took on a taint of degradation. No self-respecting man cared to engage in them, since they were now for the most part assigned to slaves.

Of the moral corruption of the age too dark a picture has sometimes been drawn. Until recent times we had no other sources of information than the classical literature, which deals almost wholly with the life of the upper classes. Among the idle rich of that time, as of most others, vices of the grossest kind were rampant, and if all Pagan society had been infected with them it would soon have collapsed through its own rottenness. But there is evidence that the mass of the people still valued and practised the virtues of a simpler age. The numerous epitaphs that have come down to us bear witness to honest, industrious lives. Private letters, of which many thousands have been recovered, amply prove that domestic affections were as pure and strong as they are to-day. Even among the corrupt aristocracy, as we know from the correspondence of such men as Pliny and Seneca, there were many shining examples of kindness and heroism. It is certain, however, that the moral sense was everywhere growing weaker, and this was fully recognized by the more earnest minds of the time. The chief cause of this decline was the falling away of the old religious sanctions. In that enlightened age it was no longer possible to believe the ancient myths. Educated men had learned to treat them as a matter of jest, and this sceptical attitude was now shared by the people at large. Augustus, himself a man of very free opinions, had perceived that the decay of religion would soon undermine the moral foundations of society. He devoted himself in his later years to the task of vitalizing the old Roman religion, and for this purpose built innumerable temples, and enlisted in his crusade the great poets and artists of the day. But no attempt to galvanize a dead religion into new life has ever been successful, and the old Paganism was dead, although in deference to the emperor men observed

FIRST AGE OF CHRISTIANITY 39

its outward forms. Yet it must not be supposed that the age was utterly without religion. Not so long ago this was taken for granted, and the success of Christianity was often explained from this point of view. Religion, it was said, had disappeared, leaving a great void in human life. The new faith rushed into this vacuum which craved to be filled again. But all experience teaches us that a mood of blank infidelity is the least fitted to respond to any religious influence. If the Apostles had laboured in a completely irreligious age they would have sown their seed upon the rock. The truth is, as we can now perceive in the light of many evidences, that it was a religious age. A generation or two before there had been a real danger that the world would sink into materialism, and at that time there would have been little opportunity for the Christian mission. But in the interval there had been a spiritual revival, which had come about through agencies that had nothing in common with the futile reforms of Augustus.

It had been partly due to the work of philosophical teachers. Stoicism, in particular, with its severe and lofty morality, had made a strong appeal to the practical Roman mind. According to Stoicism there is a principle of Reason immanent in all things and becoming conscious of itself in man. Our task as men is to bring our individual reason into harmony with this universal reason. The Stoics did not profess to offer a religion; their aim, indeed, was to help men to a rule of action which should be quite independent of religion. But the philosophy was practised, at least by many of its adherents, in a truly religious spirit. In their own lives and in the lives of their fellow men they tried to make it a substitute for the old beliefs which were no longer tenable. Stoic teachers, convinced that the chief need of the time was for spiritual guidance, used to travel about from place to place and lecture in popular fashion to all who cared to listen. Paul and his companions adopted the methods and to some extent the ideas of these Stoic missionaries, who had prepared the way for them by kindling a genuine aspiration towards a higher life.

But along with the philosophical movement there was a directly religious one. The East has always been the home of great religions, and under Roman dominion the East had been drawn into close intercourse with the West. Merchants and soldiers from Syria and Asia Minor continued, wherever they were, to practice their native forms of worship. Through Oriental slaves the foreign beliefs found entrance into every household. Those Eastern religions were all of a similar type, so much so that they could borrow freely from each other and blend together. Originating as they did in nature worship they all centred in the mysterious revival of vegetation after the blight of winter. This annual miracle had given rise to a myth which assumed a different form in each of the religions, but in its main outline was invariably the same. A young and beautiful divinity—Adonis or Attis or Serapis—was slain by a cruel enemy,

FIRST AGE OF CHRISTIANITY 41

and was lamented by a goddess, representing the fruitful earth, who was his wife or mother. At last, in answer to her prayers and ministrations, he was restored to life. Ideas of a spiritual nature had gradually woven themselves into this primitive myth and the symbolical rites in which it was embodied. The aim of the worshipper was to attain to a mood of ecstasy, in which he could feel himself identified with the god and so emerge with him into a new life. This experience was only granted to chosen initiates, who were admitted, after a period of ascetic discipline, to the "mysteries," the secret celebration in which the dying and rising of the god were exhibited in dramatic action. For the people of the West these "mystery-religions" possessed a strange fascination. They were mixed up with many superstitions, often gross and revolting, but at the heart of them was a profound spiritual idea. They answered to the feeling, deeply implanted in every human being, that his soul belongs to a higher world and must seek deliverance from the bondage of earthly and material things. It was not only the ignorant multitude that was moved and attracted by the Oriental cults with their fantastic and often childish ritual. Thoughtful men and women, who had despaired of finding true satisfaction in any philosophy, sometimes fell back on them, and interpreted the myths in the light of their deepest speculations on life and death. We are now beginning to see that the prevalence of those mystery-religions was a factor of prime importance in the spread of Christianity. Their teachings were at some points strikingly similar to those of the gospel, and for this reason, as we shall see at a later stage, had an important influence on Christian thought. Mystical and sacramental elements which had no place in the original message of Jesus, gradually found entrance by way of the Eastern cults.

In spite, therefore, of the decay of the old Paganism a new religious life was stirring in the Roman world. Its presence as yet was hardly visible to a superficial observer. The mystery religions were allowed no public recognition, and often incurred the suspicion or open hostility of the State. For the ancient mind religion was always allied with the civic consciousness. The god was the patron of the city or country, and in his worship the citizens found a bond which united them and inspired them with a fervid patriotism. This was markedly so in Rome itself, where no distinction was made between the religious and the political life. The chief magistrates were at the same time, during their term of office, the priests of the state religion. It was one of the most striking features of the new Eastern cults that they appealed to the individual, irrespective of his race or country. Their tendency, as Roman statesmen were not slow to recognize, was to draw men away from national interests and concentrate them on the task of personal salvation. They were useless for the purpose which Augustus had in view when he tried to make religion the binding force in his empire. A form of worship was devised in the course of the first

FIRST AGE OF CHRISTIANITY 43

century which aimed at achieving that end. Since the countries had now been gathered into one all-inclusive state the emperor himself, as its head and representative, was set up as a divinity. Temples were built and festivals were held in his honour, and all loyal citizens were required to observe certain forms of adoration. It was this transference to a man, and often a man of very doubtful character, of the worship due to God alone which aroused the horror of the early Christians and forced them into conflict with the ruling power. In later times the practice of Caesar-worship has often been pointed to as the crowning proof of the hopeless degradation into which the Roman world had fallen. Yet when we take due account of ancient sentiment it is fully intelligible. No clear distinction was made in Paganism between gods and superhuman men, and of all men the emperor, who wielded an illimitable power, might seem to hold the rank of a divinity. Moreover among all the subject races there was a feeling of genuine gratitude and veneration for Rome, the great peacemaker, to which all men had learned to look for protection and well-being. The emperor did in actual fact bestow the blessings which they had formerly implored from their national gods. It must not be supposed that Caesar-worship was a religion in the proper sense. The festivals held at stated seasons in honor of Rome and the emperor were supplementary to those of the various religions. They gave expression to the communal feeling, and never professed to do anything more.

But even so the imperial cult had a deep significance. We can see from it that the world was realizing its need for a religion in which all men could unite. The empire, for all its wonderful achievements, was a body without a soul. It was seeking for a spiritual unity which should correspond with the material unity. Caesar-worship was only a sorry makeshift, and of this all thinking men were well aware. But it pointed forward to the universal religion which was finally to offer itself in Christianity.

CHAPTER II

THE GOSPEL RECORD

For our knowledge of the life of Jesus we are dependent almost wholly on the New Testament. It has often appeared strange that no writer outside of the church has anything to say of the wonderful story until nearly a century afterwards. The Gospel record, we are told, is not supported by any unprejudiced testimony and must therefore be put aside as doubtful. But the silence of the Greek and Roman historians is easily explained. Acquainted as they must have been with the Christian movement, for it was widely extended before the end of the first century, they did not consider it worthy of serious notice. It is only in very recent times that our own writers abandoned that false conception of "the dignity of history," which led them to disdain all matters that only concerned the life of the common people. John Wesley, as every one can now recognize, was by far the greatest force in eighteenth century England, but the older historians make no mention of him. Occupied as they are with the wars and politics which at the time seemed all-important they never glance at the revival movement which was going on among the obscure multitude. It is not surpris-

46 FIRST AGE OF CHRISTIANITY

ing that the classical writers take a similar attitude towards the progress of Christianity.

The silence of Josephus, the Jewish historian, who wrote about 90 A.D., is more remarkable. He composed a full chronicle of events in Palestine during the very period when Jesus appeared, but says nothing of Jesus himself.[1] This cannot have been due to ignorance, for he wrote at a time when the new teaching was the subject of bitter controversy in all Jewish circles. Nor can it have been due to any blindness to the importance of the work of Jesus. All over the empire the Christian movement was now making rapid headway, and intelligent Jews, however much they might dislike it, were well aware that nothing of such world-wide interest had ever come out of Palestine. For that part Josephus does indirectly touch on the Gospel history. He devotes a chapter to the career of John the Baptist, whose greatness he acknowledges, and refers to James, who fell a victim to mob violence shortly before the siege of Jerusalem as "the brother of Jesus, the so-called Christ." Why does he say nothing of Jesus himself? His silence may perhaps be explained by the hatred which he felt, as an orthodox Jew, for the heretical teaching, though if this were his motive we might have expected him to speak violently against it. More likely, he was too well acquainted with the historical facts to repeat the slanders which were current among the Jewish and Roman readers whom he had in view.

---

[1] The one passage which alludes to Jesus has almost certainly been inserted by a Christian copyist.

FIRST AGE OF CHRISTIANITY 47

His account of John the Baptist is sympathetic, and anything he might have said of Jesus could hardly have been less so. But he knew that any favorable notice of Jesus would be displeasing to his public, and preferred to say nothing.

From non-Christian sources, therefore, we have no record of the beginning of Christianity until we come to Tacitus, the Roman historian, who wrote about 116 A.D. In his account of the fire of Rome under Nero, in the year 64 A.D., he tells how the emperor sought to divert attention from himself to the Christians, and takes occasion, in a memorable passage, to touch on the origin of their religion. "They take their name from one Christus, who was put to death in the reign of Tiberius by the procurator Pontius Pilatus, and the pestilent superstition was checked for a time. Afterwards it began to break out afresh, not only in Judaea, where the mischief first arose, but also at Rome, to which all criminal or shameful things flow in from every quarter, and find a welcome."[2] When Tacitus wrote the Roman government had become definitely hostile to the new religion, and the historian reflects the official sentiment. One thing only he cares to know about Jesus—that he was put to death after a formal trial by a Roman magistrate and must therefore have been guilty of some grave crime. This, we cannot doubt, was the fixed idea of the governing classes at Rome, jealous for the repute of Roman justice.

When we turn to Christian literature we nat-

[2] Tacitus, Ann. xv., 44.

urally look for full information on the life of Jesus, but here again we are disappointed. After the Crucifixion, as we shall see later, the interest of the church was transferred from Jesus as he had lived on earth to Jesus risen and glorified. Paul and the later New Testament writers are intensely loyal to Jesus, but for this very reason they feel it unnecessary to dwell on the circumstances of his earthly life. Jesus for them is still living, and is presently to return. He is so real to them as an actual presence that they do not need to dwell on the memory of what he has been. So general was this feeling in the primitive church that the preservation of any record of the life of Jesus is a matter for wonder. It was probably due to three main causes. (1) From the outset the church had taken the teaching of Jesus as "the Way," the practical rule for his followers, and much of the teaching was inseparable from incidents which had called it forth. His words could not be understood without some record of his actions. (2) The Christian message centred in the belief that Jesus had been truly the Messiah. In order to prove his claim it was necessary to describe certain outstanding facts about his life, which gave clear fulfilment to the prophecies of Scripture. (3) Although the earthly life was allowed to fall into the background there was one episode in it which was fundamental to the Christian faith. Jesus had died for man's redemption; everything else depended on that supreme fact. It was therefore essential to tell how he had died, how the death had been brought about, how it stood related to the life that had gone before. Almost half of each of our present Gospels is occupied with the story of the Passion and its attendant circumstances. This, we cannot doubt, was the nucleus of the whole story as it has come down to us.

Our knowledge of the life of Jesus, then, is virtually confined to the four Gospels. It is true that besides these Gospels contained in the New Testament we possess a number of others, mostly in a fragmentary condition, which came into existence early in the second century. Only one of them, the so-called Gospel of the Hebrews, bears the least evidence of resting on any authentic tradition. It is clear that after the end of the first century the memories of the actual life had grown vague and scanty. Everything of any value had been incorporated in our New Testament Gospels, and later writers could do nothing but borrow from them, and fill them out with fanciful additions.

To some extent this is true even of our Fourth Gospel, attributed in the church tradition to the Apostle John. The true authorship of this wonderful book is a many-sided problem, which will have to be considered later. But whoever wrote it had undoubtedly the three other Gospels before him and has constantly drawn on them, although he is still in a position to add valuable data which have come to him from other sources. The chief value of the Fourth Gospel is not historical but religious. Its author has pondered on the life of Jesus, and sets himself to interpret it in the light

D

of certain great ideas of his own. His work, more than any other, has helped us to understand the life in its permanent meaning, but as a historical source it needs always to be treated with some reserve.

Our main documents are therefore the Gospels of Matthew, Mark and Luke, commonly known as the Synoptic Gospels, since their contents can be arranged in parallel columns and compared together. Between these Gospels there is manifestly a very close relation, and in many passages they repeat each other almost word for word. At the same time they constantly differ, and must be regarded as independent works. On what theory of their origin can their agreements and differences be both explained? This is the "Synoptic Problem," the most difficult and also the most important of all literary problems. During the last century, and especially in the last fifty years it has been studied with endless patience and ingenuity by hundreds of scholars, who have recognized that our whole understanding of the life of Jesus is bound up with its solution.

One fact is hardly open to question—that the Gospels were composed in Greek, as we now have them, and were based on documents which were also in Greek. This is apparent from their constant verbal agreement, which cannot be set down to mere coincidence. At the same time there is sufficient proof that much of the material, perhaps all of it, originally existed in Aramaic, which was the language of Palestine. The structure of the

FIRST AGE OF CHRISTIANITY 51

sentences is Aramaic; peculiar Aramaic idioms can often be detected; and in not a few places it is fairly certain that the writer has missed the true meaning of some Aramaic word or phrase. Another fact which has been fully established by critical enquiry is that our evangelists made use of written sources. Formerly it was supposed that they committed to writing a narrative which had hitherto come down by word of mouth. This theory seemed to account in quite a natural way at once for their general agreement and for their frequent differences. It is open, however, to the fatal objection that each of the writers is able to change at will the order of his narrative, and sometimes to make long insertions and then take up the thread at the point where he left off. This he could only do if he was working with written documents.

What was the nature of these documents? It was suggested, a century ago, that they consisted of a large number of separate notes, which were finally collected and pieced together. Various followers of Jesus, according to this theory, had jotted down incidents and sayings which they remembered, and the work of the evangelists was to weave these brief memoirs into a continuous whole. There is probably much truth in this theory, but it cannot have been our evangelists who did the collecting and arranging of the scattered notes. All of them present their material in the same general order, and often place three or four unconnected passages in just the same sequence. They must have dealt with a collection already made.

We are thus shut up to two alternatives. (1) Our three evangelists all made use of a primitive Gospel which has now been lost. (2) One of our existing Gospels is the original one, and has served as the basis and model of the other two. On the ground of a minute analysis scholars are now agreed on the second alternative. It is indeed possible that there was a written Gospel prior to any that we now possess, but there can be no doubt that the earliest of our Gospels is that of Mark, and that Matthew and Luke made use of it. When the three Gospels are placed in parallel columns, with Mark in the middle, it can be shown that Matthew and Luke, however they differ from each other, always tend to agree with Mark. If one of them breaks away the other follows him, and vice versa. They have worked independently of each other, but they have both taken Mark as their authority. That Mark is earliest is further proved by his less polished language and his more primitive type of thought.

This result that Mark is the oldest Gospel is of the utmost importance, since it gives us a criterion for judging between our different accounts of the life of Christ. Whenever they seem at variance with each other it is usually safe to take our guidance from Mark. There is certainly the possibility that Matthew and Luke have corrected and amplified the narrative of Mark from other trustworthy sources. But since they depend on him we may accept his record of any given incident as the best attested. He is entitled to the preference which we always accord to the first-hand witness.

This brings us, however, to another aspect of the Synoptic Problem. Matthew and Luke are both about twice the length of Mark; whence did they derive the additional half of their material? One striking fact at once comes into prominence when we examine that part of their work which is not based on Mark. It consists in the main of things which Jesus said, as contrasted with his actions. Mark is chiefly occupied with narrative; Matthew and Luke combine this narrative with an account of the teaching. We discover further that the teaching is very largely the same in both Gospels. In each of them there are over two hundred verses in which the same sayings are reported, often in identical words. The inference is that along with Mark they made use of a work now lost which was composed almost entirely of sayings of Jesus. Probably it never obtained fixity as a regular book. It was rather a loose collection which was current in various forms, and might be revised or added to. The church dealt with it, to use a rough analogy, as it now does with its collection of hymns. Each community makes its own hymnal, suitable to its own needs, so that there is no uniform book; yet all the books are composed for the most part of the same material. The sayings of Jesus seem likewise to have circulated in a number of versions, and that which Matthew knew differed considerably in extent and contents from that of Luke.

But a large nucleus was necessarily the same in all versions.

This compendium of Jesus' teaching, (which modern scholars have agreed to designate by the symbol Q), may fairly be regarded as the oldest stratum in the Gospel tradition. Mark himself appears to make use of it, though in a much more restricted way than the two later evangelists. Words escape the memory far more easily than facts, and it must have become apparent almost from the first that if the teaching of Jesus was not to be forgotten it must be put down in writing. This was all the more necessary as the church had adopted the teaching as its practical rule. It required to have the sayings in some definite form about which there could be no dispute.

Mark and Q are the main strands in the composition of our Gospels, but a third part of Matthew and a still larger part of Luke can be assigned to neither of them. Luke himself tells us in the dedication of his Gospel that "many have taken in hand to draw up a narrative concerning those matters which have been fulfilled among us," [3] and indicates that he has availed himself of all those records. One of them was pretty certainly an extended document, and was particularly rich in parables and illustrative anecdotes. It is his inclusion of this document which gives distinctive value to the work of Luke. We know nothing of its purpose and origin, but it clearly goes back to a time when the memory of Jesus was still fresh and

[3] Lk. i. 1-4.

vivid. It enables us better than any of the other narratives to realize the charm of his personality and the attractive power of his teaching.

When we have separated all that can reasonably be assigned to written sources a residuum is left which can only be accounted for by oral tradition. Some of the anecdotes which were still circulated by word of mouth fifty or sixty years after Jesus' death may well be authentic, but it is obvious that they stand on a different level from those which were written down, soon after the event. Matthew and Luke, for instance, preface their Gospels with an account of marvellous circumstances which attended Jesus' birth, and near the close they tell of similar portents at the time of the Crucifixion. To question the accuracy of these additions does not imply any disbelief in the Gospel history. When Mark or Q is our authority we can feel that we are standing on solid historical ground, while information that has come down by vague oral report must be carefully scrutinized. The chief task of the modern historian of the life of Jesus is to examine the sources and so arrive at valid conclusions as to the facts.

From this brief outline it is possible to form to ourselves some conception of how the Gospels came to be written. At the outset the church felt no need of documents. The disciples who had consorted with Jesus were still living, and his story as told by these eye-witnesses was far more interesting and convincing than any book could make it. Even in those early days, however, the practice arose of jotting down stray sayings of Jesus which might otherwise be lost. Short collections of the sayings were made, and were gradually brought together in the compendium of his teaching which we call Q. For the narrative of Jesus' life and death the church was still dependent on oral testimony, but as the eye-witnesses passed away it became evident that their record would soon disappear unless it was committed to writing. About the year 70 A.D. (the precise date cannot be determined) this work was undertaken by Mark. According to a notice in one of the earliest Fathers he was a companion of Peter and composed his record from reminiscences of the Apostle's teaching. Others who had listened to the Apostles drew up similar records about the same time or shortly afterwards. Finally, towards the close of the century it occurred to two men, independently of each other, to combine the account of Jesus' life with that of his teaching. They went about their work in different ways. Matthew divides Mark into five sections, between each of which he introduces a discourse, made up of a number of sayings from Q skilfully selected and woven together. Luke is less systematic. Sometimes he blends the narrative and the sayings; at one place he leaves Mark entirely to one side for nine chapters together (ix. 51–xviii. 14), and brings in a variety of material which he has found in Q and his other sources. The aim of Luke is to write a biography, as full and interesting as he can make it. Matthew's aim is more practical. He sets himself to draw up a

FIRST AGE OF CHRISTIANITY 57

manual of Christian instruction, in which all the facts about Jesus' life and teaching may be learned in convenient form.

The importance of these critical results can hardly be emphasized too much. It has often been argued that since the evangelists, to whom we owe all our knowledge of the life of Jesus, wrote more than half a century after the event, we can place little reliance on their testimony. Until modern times this argument was almost unanswerable, and caused the gravest misgivings in many devout minds. As a result of the critical enquiry it has now lost its force. It has been demonstrated, by a purely scientific analysis, that although the Gospels are themselves late they are compiled from records which were drawn up much earlier, and which run back, in their main elements, to the years immediately following the Lord's death. Criticism has indeed made it clear that in our Gospels there are various strata, some of them of less historical value than others. But in its large result it has been constructive. We can now accept, not merely by an act of faith but on the ground of strict historical evidence, the essential facts concerning the life of Christ.

CHAPTER III

THE LIFE OF JESUS

(1) THE EARLIER LIFE

The life of Jesus was not only the greatest of which we have any record, but in one sense it is better known to us than any other. Jesus stands before us so clearly, in the Gospel story, that millions of his followers have been able to realize him as an actual presence. They can discern not only the things he did but the thoughts and purposes which gave meaning to his actions. Yet no biography of Jesus, in the proper sense of the term, can ever be written. The Gospel narratives cover only that short closing period when he was engaged in his public ministry. Their record even of this year or two is obscure and fragmentary. Half of it is occupied with his death and the events that accompanied it, and for the rest we have only a few disconnected anecdotes.

Mark, the earliest evangelist, only begins his narrative with the opening of the ministry, and leaves us to infer what had gone before from several incidental allusions.[1] Matthew and Luke both devote two introductory chapters to the marvelous circumstances of Jesus' birth, but this portion of their record, while it embodies traditions which

---
[1] Mk. iv. 31-35; vi. 3.

FIRST AGE OF CHRISTIANITY 59

had long been current in the church, does not appear to rest on written documents, and has doubtful historical value. It is significant that the two accounts, agreeing as they do on certain main facts, contradict one another on almost every point of detail.

There can be little doubt that Jesus was born towards the close of the reign of Herod, who died in 4 B. C. The year of his birth is, however, uncertain. According to Luke he was "about thirty years old" when he began his ministry in 26 or 27 A. D.[2] Luke does not pretend to know his precise age and uses a vague phrase which merely indicates that he was past his first youth. His birth may have fallen in 4 B. C., or, more probably, several years before.

Matthew and Luke both give a genealogy of Jesus, proving that he was descended from David and so fulfilled the Old Testament predictions of the Messiah. The two genealogies are at variance with each other and cannot both be authentic. It does not follow that the main fact of the descent from David must be set aside. We can well believe that the family had always cherished the memory of its illustrious origin, even though some of the obscure links had been forgotten in the course of a thousand years. Paul also mentions the fact of the Davidic descent of Jesus as accepted by every one in the early church,[3] and apparently it was not challenged by the outside world. It is noticeable

---
[2] Lk. iii. 23.
[3] Rom. i. 3.

that in both genealogies the descent is traced through Joseph and not through Mary. This can hardly be explained on any other ground than that they date from a period which knew nothing of the Virgin Birth. For the New Testament writers generally the manner of Jesus' birth has none of the religious importance which has sometimes been attached to it. That he was born of a Virgin is only stated by Matthew and in one verse of Luke, which may possibly have been inserted by a later hand.[4] It must be noted, too, that the birth stories are on a different footing from the later part of the record. When they come to deal with Jesus' ministry Matthew and Luke make use of written sources which go back to an early date and have undoubted historical value. In the opening chapters they rely on popular traditions, which we have no means of testing.

The one incident which has come down to us out of the early life of Jesus is that of his visit to the temple, when, as a boy of twelve, he entered on his full privileges and obligations as a member of the Jewish race.[5] That the anecdote is authentic we may well believe, for in its naturalness and simplicity it has nothing in common with the legendary stories which gathered at a later time around the Infancy. We learn from it that even as a boy Jesus was preoccupied with the great questions of religion, and welcomed the opportunity of listening to the famous teachers at Jerusalem, who on

---
[4] Lk. i. 34.
[5] Lk. ii. 41 ff.

FIRST AGE OF CHRISTIANITY 61

their side were charmed by his youthful intelligence and earnestness. Perhaps it was on this occasion that the consciousness of a divine calling first awoke in him. "Know ye not," he is reported to have asked in the temple, "that I must be in my Father's house?"

Jewish religion was based on the Scriptures, and as a result of this the Jews were an educated people. A school was attached to every synagogue, where children were instructed in the sacred books by which their lives were to be guided. Jesus would receive this customary education. We know from his recorded teaching that the Psalms and Prophets had become a living part of his own mind. Not only his thought but his language has a beauty and elevation due to his early familiarity with a great literature. At Nazareth, too, although it was an obscure town in a small province, he had opportunities of contact with the larger world of his time. The main highroad from the East, stretching between Syria and Egypt, lay close to the town, which also overlooked the plain of Esdraelon, with its memories of a hundred battles. The parables of Jesus, so wonderful in their variety and their wide knowledge of human life, owed much to these early surroundings.

Joseph was a carpenter, and the eldest son, as is customary in the East, was apprenticed to the same trade. We can infer from Mark's silence as to the father, when the family is mentioned, that Joseph was dead before the opening of the ministry. Probably for a considerable time Jesus had been himself the Carpenter. His occupation has often been pictured as a lowly one, in which he had grown embittered with a sense of social injustice; but this view, it is almost certain, is quite a false one. In the simple society of Nazareth the carpenter would hold an honored position. Our Gospels lay stress on the sacrifice which Jesus had made when he gave up his home and livelihood to become teacher and companion of the poor.

All the time that he worked as a carpenter at Nazareth, Jesus must have been pondering deeply on the great questions of religion and life. Nothing impresses us more as we study his teaching than the maturity of all his thoughts and the tranquil assurance with which he utters them. Such teaching, we may be sure, was not improvised. For years he had been preparing himself for his great work and was only waiting for some clear sign that would call him to it. The sign was at last given him by the appearance of John the Baptist, announcing that the Kingdom of God was at hand.

The idea of the Kingdom was one which had always possessed the higher minds in Israel. Its origin is perhaps to be sought in the widespread belief, derived from Babylonian astronomy and familiar to us through the poetry of Greece and Rome, that the world had begun with a Golden Age to which it would at last return when the cycle of ages had run its course. The Hebrew thinkers had interpreted this belief in the light of great religious ideas. They held that the present age, in which evil was triumphant, was hastening

FIRST AGE OF CHRISTIANITY 63

to an end, and would give place to a new age in which God alone would reign. The hope of a better time, when the world of nature would be renewed and disease and poverty disappear, merged itself in the hope of the final victory of righteousness. It was combined, too, with hope for the nation. Amidst the calamities of the present the prophets looked forward to that future age when Israel would be delivered from all enemies and take its rightful place as the favored people of God. In the period which had elapsed since the exile the hope had grown more intense and had, at the same time, taken a peculiar direction. The long-continued troubles had created a general mood of pessimism. A belief had grown up that God had surrendered the world for the time being to the powers of wickedness. The prophets had declared that in spite of evil the forces of righteousness were at work and would finally conquer; but this faith seemed no longer possible. Evil had so entrenched itself that a better time could only come through miracle. God must Himself interpose, destroy the old order entirely, and replace it by a new one in which his will would prevail. Sometimes it was assumed that He would act directly; sometimes He was conceived as acting through the Messiah, who was pictured as an angelic being, suddenly appearing from heaven.

John took up the hope of the Kingdom of God, and by his striking personality and fervent utterance gave it a new reality. In language modelled on that of the ancient prophets he declared that the long-expected day was just at hand. He called on men, in view of its coming, to reform their lives, and offered them baptism in the river Jordan as a pledge that they had repented and were thus fit to enter the Kingdom. The greatness of John consisted in this uniting of the thought of the Kingdom with a moral demand. Others had held out the hope of a better age as a comfort and encouragement to the people in their troubles. John found in it the motive power for a moral reformation. A crisis was near; all men would presently be brought to judgment; none would be admitted to the Kingdom but those who were declared righteous. For all, therefore, it was a matter of life and death to change their lives before they were summoned before the Judge.

The mission of John seems only to have lasted a few months altogether, but in that short time he made a deep impression. From all parts of the country people thronged to his hermitage on the east bank of the Jordan and received his baptism. A body of disciples formed around him and continued his work long after his death. It has sometimes been maintained that Jesus was originally one of those disciples, and that the vital relation of John to the later movement has purposely been minimized in our records. But the truth is almost certainly the other way. Our Gospel writers in their anxiety to make out that John was the forerunner of Jesus have given us to understand that the connection between them was much closer than it really was. They have failed to recognize that

FIRST AGE OF CHRISTIANITY 65

John was a great religious leader in his own right, and that his movement was separate from that of Jesus. He appears to have met with Jesus only once, on the occasion of the Baptism, and to have then seen in him nothing more than one of the inquiring multitude.

That incident of the Baptism is beset with many difficulties, but this much at least seems clear. During the silent years at Nazareth Jesus had been meditating on the divine purposes and in the message of John he found a response to his own deep convictions. He made a journey to the wilderness beside the Jordan to hear the new prophet, and sought baptism at his hands. In the moment of his baptism he underwent a decisive experience, in which the thoughts and surmises which had long been gathering in his mind were suddenly crystallized. It was revealed to him that he was called to a supreme work, that he stood in a unique relation to God. The consciousness that he was himself the Messiah does not seem to have dawned on him till a later time, but from the moment of the baptism he knew himself to be set apart by God.

Under the stress of this high experience he withdrew for a while into the wilderness to ponder on his call. The story of the Temptation is told in figurative language, but we can gather from it that he passed through a terrible inward conflict. He was allured by one plan and another whereby he might accomplish his work for God swiftly and easily, but in the end he put them all aside and chose the slow and difficult path. He perceived that in the task to which he had set himself he must rely solely on spiritual forces. All other methods, however plausible, were of the evil one.

His resolve thus made he returned to Galilee and began a public mission. John in the interval had been thrown into prison by Herod Antipas, who feared, as Josephus tells us, that his influence with the people might lead to a revolt. This was doubtless the king's true motive, though it was strengthened by his private grudge against the prophet, who had denounced him for his immoral life. From the outset, therefore, Jesus had clear warning of the danger to which he exposed himself by his mission. It has often been taken for granted that he commenced his work under bright auspices and never suspected till near the end that he would meet with disaster. But at no time can he thus have misjudged his prospects. The fate of John was always before his eyes, and he knew that sooner or later he must expect to suffer likewise.

(2) The Ministry

John had called on men to repent since the Kingdom of God was at hand, and Jesus took up the message. He proclaimed it to all who cared to listen as he made his way northward along the shore of the lake of Galilee. John had taken his abode in a solitary place and had required the people to seek him out. Jesus from the first adopted a different method. He never tried to strike the popular imagination by strange dress or language or manner of life. He mingled with the people as

FIRST AGE OF CHRISTIANITY 67

one of them in their market-places and synagogues. For some time he seems to have attracted little attention, but gradually he made a few adherents. The first were two pairs of brothers, Simon and Andrew, James and John, who were so strongly drawn to him that they gave up their trade as fishermen and became his companions and helpers. Simon was a married man, with a house of his own at Capernaum, and here he took Jesus as his guest. During the mission in Galilee Capernaum was henceforth his centre. Much of his work was done in this little town and the villages adjoining it, and from Capernaum, situated as it was in the middle of the province, he made frequent journeys by land and water. For the greater part of his public career he was occupied with this work in Galilee.

Two questions of primary importance here present themselves, and neither of them can be definitely answered. (1) What was the duration of Jesus' ministry? The Fourth Gospel seems to allow for a period of something like three years, though the computation is doubtful. The Synoptic Gospels clearly assume a much shorter period, but never define it. On one occasion they tell of the disciples passing through the ripe corn-fields,[6] and since the harvest in Palestine falls at the Passover season there must have been at least one Passover in Jesus' ministry before the closing one at Jerusalem. On this ground it has been calculated that he may have worked for about eighteen months in all. The other question is still more

---
[6] Mt. xii. 1; Mk. ii. 23; Lk. vi. 1.

important and more difficult to answer. (2) What was the plan which Jesus set before him? When he began his work in Galilee did he intend that this should continue to be his sphere, or did he contemplate a larger and perhaps world-wide mission to which the early one should be preparatory? It may be that he had no definite plan and was content to start the work and leave its later development in the hands of God. Or perhaps he had some plan in his mind which was not to come to fruition. We must never forget as we study his life, that it was cut off in mid-career. From what he did in the brief period which was granted him we can only guess at the larger intention that was in his mind.

That he contemplated a work on some greater scale may be inferred from his call of twelve disciples, soon after his settlement in Capernaum. His object, Mark tells us, was twofold—"that they should be with him and that he should send them out to preach."[7] The first object he achieved. By daily intercourse with the disciples he so imbued them with his own spirit that through them it became a leavening power in the world. But during his lifetime he never, except in a very limited sense, employed them as missionaries. His calling of them seems to point to some larger aim which he did not live to accomplish.

From the time of his settlement at Capernaum Jesus began to make a singular impression, which was all the greater as he never sought by any sen-

---
[7] Mk. iii. 14.

FIRST AGE OF CHRISTIANITY 69

sational methods to secure the world's notice. As men observed at the time he carefully avoided all self-advertisement.[8] He attracted and subdued them by an inherent power which they were unable to explain. It was chiefly as a teacher that he made his influence felt, and his teaching won attention not only by its substance but by the charm and originality of its form. He had the gift of driving home a great truth by a vivid and unforgettable phrase. He illustrated his thought with an endless wealth of parables, drawn from nature and human life, so that the most ignorant understood him and listened to him with delight. Above all, his teaching carried with it the stamp of authority.[9] Men felt that he spoke what he knew by immediate insight—that he was a voice and not an echo.

The effect produced by his teaching was enhanced by his miracles. That he performed actions which seemed to the on-lookers miraculous cannot be doubted, in view of the Gospel evidence; but certain considerations have always to be borne in mind. (1) The age was not a scientific one, and events we should now set down to natural causes were often regarded as miracles. (2) There was a tendency as time went on to accentuate the marvelous element in the work of Jesus. Of this we have many proofs when we compare the narratives in Mark with those in the later Gospels. (3) Some of the miracles, especially those in which Jesus controls the forces of nature, have plainly a symbolical

---
[8] Mt. xii. 16 ff.
[9] Mk. i. 23.

value. The facts, whatever they may have been, are subordinated to the spiritual idea. It is hard to say whether the incident is miracle or parable. (4) The miraculous element had a far smaller place in the life of Jesus than we might infer from our Gospels. It is clear from their own testimony that he disliked the reputation of a wonder-worker, which tended to distract men's minds from his teaching. When he put forth his power he always did so reluctantly, and often with the express injunction that no one should be told.[10] The miracles were not the outstanding feature of his work but were only wrought occasionally.

By far the largest group of miracles, and those which are best attested, are the healings, and these healings, when we examine them have almost all to do with some form of mental disease. According to the superstitious ideas of that time all nervous maladies were ascribed to demons, which had dislodged the true personality. Jesus cast out the demons. His word and touch and presence acted miraculously on darkened souls and restored them to health. That he did exert this healing power is a fact that cannot be doubted, and from this may have arisen the belief that he had sovereignty even on earth over all the forces hostile to man.

However we may explain these narratives, and all explanations are only guess-work, it is significant that men thought of him, while he mingled with them in familiar intercourse, as one who could work miracles. Their attitude towards him, as we

---
[10] Mt. viii. 4; xii. 16; Mk. viii. 26.

FIRST AGE OF CHRISTIANITY 71

can gather from the whole tenor of the Gospels, was not merely one of admiration, as for a great teacher and prophet, but one of awe. They felt that he was a man apart from others, that he carried with him a divine power. Sometimes in the crowd that listened to him there would be hysterical persons who expressed this feeling in a wild cry of adoration,[11] but it was present in all, and even in his enemies. It was this sense that he was something more than man which gave meaning to his forgiveness, his sympathy, his tenderness to the poor and outcast. All suffering souls were helped by him because they knew that he was not like other men. He made real to them by his own action the love and mercy of God.

From Capernaum as a centre he made journeys over Galilee, proclaiming his message sometimes in synagogues, sometimes in fields or on hillsides or in houses where he was a guest. The report of him had now spread over the country, and wherever he went he was followed by enthusiastic crowds. But with his growing fame he was exposed to ever-growing danger. The Pharisees had from the first looked on him doubtfully, and their attitude soon became one of open hostility. They tried in vain to detect him in some clear breach of the Law, of which they had constituted themselves the guardians, but they rightly perceived that the whole drift of his teaching was towards the displacement of the Law. There are signs, too, that from an early stage he aroused suspicions on political grounds. His work

---
[11] Mt. ix. 27; Mk. x. 28; Lk. xviii. 38.

was purely religious, and he sought by every possible means to dissociate it from the revolutionary movement. To this alone it was due that he was left so long unmolested. In Palestine, however, where national and religious feelings were so closely allied, the ruling authorities were always afraid of any popular religious movement. The chief priests at Jerusalem, who stood for the existing order, had now heard of the excitement in Galilee and had taken the alarm. While Jesus pursued his work with ever-growing success their spies were narrowly watching him. He was threatened, at the same time, by a more pressing danger. Herod Antipas had arrested John the Baptist as a popular agitator and after keeping him a considerable time in prison had put him to death. The suspicions with which he had regarded John were now turned against Jesus.

So while all the prospects were apparently growing brighter, the sky was beginning to darken. The family of Jesus seem to have guessed the peril to which he was exposed, and made an effort to withdraw him from his work, on the pretext that his reason had given way. He was warned by certain Pharisees who were friendly to him that Herod had determined to take his life.[12] It was clear to him that if his work was not to come to a futile and premature end he must escape from Herod's jurisdiction.[13] At the same time he had another motive for seeking an interval of retirement. The

---
[12] Lk. xiii. 31.
[13] Mk. vii. 24.

FIRST AGE OF CHRISTIANITY 73

outward crisis which had overtaken him coincided with an inward one.

During the whole Galilaean period he had been occupied with the thought of the Kingdom, and of himself and his own significance for the Kingdom he had said nothing. It has been suggested that he observed this silence in order to avoid a conflict with the authorities, or because he felt that the people, with their ardent hope of a national deliverer, were not yet ready to understand his purely spiritual claim. We cannot believe, however, that he would have suppressed the cardinal fact of his mission for any mere prudential motive. If he did not declare himself the simplest and most natural explanation is that he was not yet entirely clear in his own mind. Ever since his boyhood he had felt himself dedicated to some great service for God, and at his baptism he had received the call to proclaim the Kingdom. But as he proceeded in his work the conviction grew upon him that he was something more than the herald of the Kingdom. He was the destined Messiah, through whom it was to come. It was not in any spirit of presumption but with doubt and reluctance that he arrived at this assurance. The name of Messiah carried with it a tremendous responsibility from which he shrank. It was involved, too, with national and apocalyptic ideas with which he had little sympathy, and he could not accept it until he had changed its meaning. We can perceive, as we study the later period in Galilee, that a struggle was going on in his mind. Others were anxious that he should declare himself Messiah, but he drew back. On one occasion John, who heard in prison of his great work, sent two disciples to ask him plainly, "Art thou the Coming One?" and he refused to give a definite answer. Yet the conviction grew in him and could not be repressed, that he was no other than the Messiah.

Under stress of the double crisis he left Galilee with his disciples, keeping his movements secret. Departing by the shortest road out of Herod's domains he passed northward to the Phoenician coast, and seems to have spent some time in aimless wandering. He next appears on his journey southward in the neighborhood of Caesarea Philippi, near the sources of the Jordan. It was here that he at last took the decisive step.[14] His disciples had long surmised that he was no other than the Messiah, and he now admitted the claim, although he impressed on them that for the present they must keep it secret. At the same time he told them plainly that he would fulfill his Messianic calling by suffering and death. The disciples were shocked by this strange inversion of all the prophetic forecasts, and Peter declared that he must be mistaken. But Jesus sternly rebuked him. The will of God was clear and he must not be tempted to swerve from it and take any easier path.

His resolve was now made and he acted on it without delay. He laid his plans to arrive at Jerusalem for the feast of Passover which was approaching, and declare himself to the assembled

---
[14] Mk. viii. 27.

FIRST AGE OF CHRISTIANITY 75

people. After re-visiting Galilee secretly to make his final preparations he set out on his journey, travelling, it would appear, by the road that lay east of the Jordan, which it re-crossed at the fords of Jericho. Little is told of this ever-memorable journey, except that again and again he reminded the disciples that they must be prepared for the worst. Yet it is wrong to think of him as going up deliberately to die. Our view of the whole closing period has been distorted by the assumption that he knew beforehand precisely all that was going to happen. We have rather to think of him as uncertain till the very last. He was aware of the strong forces arrayed against him, and knew that in all human probability he would encounter death. He felt, too, that the highest service for God involved suffering, and that the Messiah must fulfil his task as the prophets had done before him. There was a clear presentiment in his mind that he would die at Jerusalem, but he still deemed it possible that he might be mistaken. Perhaps in some wonderful manner that he could not yet foresee God would interpose to bring his cause to victory. He was certain of nothing except that God had laid a duty on him which could only be accomplished by his appearance in Jerusalem at the great feast. He therefore went up, prepared for death, but leaving the issue in the hands of God.

It has often been supposed that in this closing period of his life he was solitary and desperate. Formerly he had been surrounded by popular enthusiasm, but the multitude, which had looked for a national deliverer, had been disappointed in him, and had now turned hostile or indifferent. This view is based on the false assumption that from the first he had put forward a claim to be Messiah, thus arousing an expectation which he had done nothing to fulfil. But from Mark's narrative it is plain that he had made no declaration outside his own company of disciples. For the people he was "Jesus, the Prophet of Nazareth," and the curiosity about him, instead of waning, was always growing stronger. A rumor was abroad that he was more than a prophet, and his chief anxiety in the later months was to restrain the popular excitement. It is only when we realize this that the closing events become intelligible. If the authorities had seen nothing in Jesus but a discredited leader, already deserted by his following, they would have left him alone. But they knew that extravagant hopes were now centred on him. He had aroused the nation and might at any moment sweep it off its feet. It is unjust to think of them merely as wicked conspirators, bent on destroying a helpless and innocent man. From their own point of view they were acting in the public interest. A movement was on foot which was rapidly becoming more dangerous, and which must be firmly dealt with before it was too late.

(3) The Passion

On his way to Jerusalem Jesus was received everywhere with the honor due to a great prophet, and entered the city in the midst of a triumphal procession. He had himself arranged the manner of his entry, partly to suggest, in the light of Old Testament prophecy, that he had come to offer himself as the Messiah, and partly, we may well believe, to secure the public attention from the very outset, and so guard himself against possible treachery. He was fully conscious of the favor which he enjoyed with the people, and was careful to use it for his protection during his few days in Jerusalem. On the day following his arrival he appeared in the temple and drove out the merchants and exchangers who had turned the holy place into a common market. This traffic in the temple, permitted and encouraged by the chief priests who made their profit from it, had long been a public scandal. When Jesus, by virtue of his moral authority, commanded it to cease, no one ventured to resist him.

His bold action, however, had been a direct challenge to the priestly authorities who had abused their sacred trust, and they at once met together to concert measures against him. It was decided at this fateful meeting that he must die; but there were grave difficulties in the way, and these must be borne in mind before we can understand the events that followed. (1) Jesus was in high favor with the people, and the multitude assembled at the Passover feast was notoriously excitable. A public arrest would be certain to bring on a serious riot, and everything must be done secretly. (2) As yet there was no valid charge on which Jesus could be put on trial. Though his teaching was plainly incompatible with the Law he had never attacked it. While he apparently intended to come forward as Messiah he had not yet made a public claim. Some definite evidence must be procured before he could be tried and condemned. (3) The consent of the Roman governor was indispensable. In matters of ordinary justice the native council, presided over by the high-priest, could act at its discretion, but no sentence of death was allowed to pass until the Roman magistrate had given his sanction. (4) The feast-day was only two or three days distant, and action could not be delayed till it was over, for the governor, who only stayed in the city during the critical week, would then have departed. Moreover the designs of Jesus were uncertain. At any moment he might take some step which would cause an outbreak, and, if possible, he must be forestalled. These were the difficulties, and arangements were now made to meet them.

Next morning, when Jesus appeared in the temple precincts, the agents of the council were awaiting him with a series of carefully prepared questions which would force him to incriminate himself. He perceived the snares and avoided them, in his answers, with marvelous skill. Meanwhile the authorities had laid their plans for a secret arrest, and here they were successful. By some means they had won over one of the disciples, Judas Iscariot, to watch the private movements of his Master and give speedy information where he could be found alone. It cannot be supposed that Jesus had any clear knowledge of the plot that was forming

FIRST AGE OF CHRISTIANITY 79

against him. Yet he was fully conscious that he was in deadly peril. He had taken his abode during his sojourn at the village of Bethany, just outside of the city, and a touching scene took place that night on his return. A woman, one of his followers, approached him as he reclined at supper, and in a passion of loyalty poured a precious ointment on his head. Some of the company murmured at her wasteful action, but he declared that she had done well. His death was approaching, and she had anointed him for his burial.

It was probably the next evening when Jesus took his last supper with his disciples. By this time he had reason to believe, on what grounds we do not know, that his death was imminent, and the little company met in an upper room, lent them by an unknown friend in Jerusalem, for a farewell meal. If we accept the Synoptic account it was the regular Passover supper, observed in every Jewish household on the evening before the great feast. It would thus follow that the Crucifixion took place on the actual Passover day, and in view of the peculiar sanctity which attached to the day this seems impossible. There is good reason to believe that the Fourth Gospel, which places the death of Jesus on the day before the Passover, has preserved the right tradition. The Last Supper, therefore, was not the Passover meal but an ordinary supper, which was invested by Jesus himself with a solemn meaning. According to Paul's account in I Cor. xi. 23-25, he instituted it as a memorial feast which should impress on his people in all succeeding times the fact of his redeeming death. The Gospels seem rather to present it as a feast of anticipation. They tell how on the eve of his death Jesus comforted his disciples with the promise that after a brief parting they would be reunited with him in the Kingdom of God.

After the Supper he returned with his followers towards Bethany, but halted, a little way out from the city, at a garden known as Gethsemane, where he prayed in an agony, "Father; all things are possible to thee: take away this cup from me; nevertheless not what I will but what thou wilt." This incident, like others in the Passion story, has often been misinterpreted through the common assumption that Jesus knew clearly beforehand all that was to happen. His agony thus appears like a breaking down at the immediate prospect of death. But the whole purpose of his prayer was to find light in a dreadful uncertainty. His one desire was to submit to the will of God, but might it not be that he had mistaken it? He could proceed no further until he was fully assured that there was no other way.

While he was still praying a band of the temple police came upon him under the guidance of Judas, who apparently had slipped away and given his information as soon as Jesus had entered the garden. The disciples made a brief resistance, but Jesus bade them look to their own safety and surrendered himself. He was first taken to the house of Annas, a former high-priest and still the leader of the Sadducaean party. After a brief examina-

FIRST AGE OF CHRISTIANITY 81

tion before this crafty politician, who had probably been the ruling spirit in the whole conspiracy, he was sent to the official residence of Caiaphas the high-priest, where the council had already gathered. Our accounts of the trial are obscure and confused, and in view of the circumstances they could hardly have been otherwise. As a Jewish court the council was obliged to try the prisoner on a religious charge, punishable under Jewish law; but its real object was to frame a case against him which could be presented to the Roman governor. The religious charge had somehow to be twisted into a political one, for otherwise no sentence could be procured. Ostensibly, therefore, Jesus was accused of blasphemy, to which the Mosaic law attached the penalty of death. Various witnesses were called, who reported sayings which he had uttered during the past few days in Jerusalem; but no two of them were found to agree. Finally, when all the evidence seemed to lead to no result, the high-priest put a direct question, "Art thou the Christ?" It was on this ground that he was a Messianic agitator that the council meant to accuse him before the governor, but the real charge had hitherto been kept in the background. Now it was suddenly sprung on Jesus, and he answered, we are told, unreservedly. "I am." He was then held to have confessed the blasphemy, and was judged worthy of death That confession before the high-priest was the one public declaration of his Messiahship that Jesus made, and it has sometimes been doubted whether the report in our Gospels is authentic. All through the trial he had refused to utter a word; would he have broken this silence to make a pronouncement which thus far he had carefully withheld, and which would certainly entail his death? But it may well be that he availed himself of what he knew would be his last opportunity. He had intended, perhaps, to make his proclamation on Passover day before the assembled multitude. This was not to be, and unless he was to leave the world with his great confession unuttered he must make it now.

Early in the morning he was led before Pilate the governor for the second and decisive trial. The accusers now took their stand solely on the Messianic charge, presenting it in such a way as to make out that he was a dangerous political agitator. Pilate called on him to speak in his own defence, but this he refused to do, aware, no doubt, that this heathen judge would never understand him. The accusers denounced him vehemently, but this violence put Pilate on his guard. He perceived that this was a case in which Jewish religious passions were involved. He perceived, too, that with all the invective no real evidence was offered. The prisoner had been guilty, at the worst, of visionary ideas, and had manifestly done nothing to disturb the peace. Pilate decided to let him go, but in order to pacify the Jewish leaders suggested that he should be formally condemned and then receive the pardon granted to a selected prisoner at the holy season. At this point the crowd in front of the judgment-seat—creatures, no doubt, of the chief priests and brought there for this very purpose—

he was trying to repeat the Psalm. More likely the words were forced from him by a suffering which had passed beyond endurance, and were his appeal to God to support him in his agony. One of the bystanders, either from pity or from some superstitious motive, touched his lips with a sponge soaked in vinegar to assuage his thirst. He revived for a moment, and then, with a sudden cry, expired. He had died long before the time which was usual in crucifixion, and perhaps his death was not wholly due to the effects of the torture following the terrible strain of the preceding days. The loud cry with which he died seems to betoken a sudden spasm, and the fourth evangelist tells us that when a spear was thrust into his side after death there issued what appeared to be mingled blood and water.[15] It has been conjectured, on medical grounds, that the immediate cause of his death was a rupture of the heart.

It was now late in the Friday afternoon, and sunset would mark the beginning of the Sabbath, which would this year be also the Passover day. Jewish sentiment required that the bodies of the victims should be removed, and an unexpected friend came forward in Joseph of Arimathaea, a man of good position who had been secretly impressed by Jesus and now requested that he might have his body for honorable burial. His petition was granted, and the body was reverently laid in a rock-hewn tomb, several women who had come up from Galilee assisting as the chief mourners.

[15] Ju. xix. 34.

FIRST AGE OF CHRISTIANITY

began to utter menacing shouts, threatening to denounce Pilate to the emperor if he acquitted this dangerous rebel. In spite of his better judgment the governor yielded and condemned Jesus to death.

Crucifixion, the ordinary form of capital punishment for all except Roman citizens, was preceded by scourging, and this torture was now inflicted on Jesus. He was then given over to a band of soldiers who treated him with brutal insult while the cross was being prepared. It was finally placed on his shoulders and he was led out, along with two convicted robbers, to a low hill known as Calvary, just outside of the city gates. At the third hour—nine in the morning—he was nailed to the Cross. As the law required, a brief inscription was placed over his head, stating the charge on which he had been sentenced. It consisted of one mocking phrase, "King of the Jews." There was a humane custom in Judaea of administering an opiate to the victims of crucifixion, and this merciful drug was offered to Jesus, but he declined it, resolving to keep his mind clear to the last. For six hours he endured the unspeakable torment. Later Christian tradition sought to fill in this dreadful interval with various incidents, but none of these can be accounted certain. Since the moment of his arrest Jesus had suffered in silence, and he maintained this silence almost to the end. Then towards the ninth hour (three in the afternoon) he cried out "Eloi, Eloi, lama sabachthani," "My God, My God, why hast thou forsaken me?" These words form the opening of the twenty-second Psalm, and it may be that

Darkness had now come on and they could not perform the usual rites of embalming, which had therefore to be left over till the Sabbath was past. A large stone was meanwhile rolled into the mouth of the tomb to preserve it from violation.

When Jesus was arrested at Gethsemane the disciples had scattered and fled. Peter alone had ventured to follow the band of captors at a distance, and had slipped into the court-yard of the highpriest's house while the trial was in process; but when he was recognized had tried to deny that he belonged to Jesus' company. From Mark's account it would appear that before the Crucifixion took place all the disciples had escaped from the city and were on their way back to Galilee. We know from their later conduct that they were men of high courage, and their momentary weakness must be set down to a panic which in the circumstances was not unnatural. The crisis had come upon them at midnight. They were Galilaean peasants, friendless in a strange city. They knew that nothing they might now do could save their Master, and believed that they themselves were exposed to the danger which had overtaken him. In spite of the explicit warnings of Jesus they had been confident to the end that he would triumph, and the sudden collapse of his cause had taken them completely by surprise. Utterly unnerved they fled and made their way homeward.

The Galilaean women, however, remained in the city, and at sunrise on the third day, as soon as it was possible to resume the duties which the Sab-

bath had interrupted, they visited the tomb, to find
the stone was rolled away and the body vanished.
"They were troubled and were amazed; neither
said they anything to any man, for they were
afraid." With these words the Gospel of Mark
abruptly ends.[16] for the twelve verses which follow are not found in the earliest manuscripts, and
were undoubtedly added by a later hand to replace
the original ending. There is no good reason to
doubt that it had been lost accidentally, but the
loss must have taken place at a very early date, for
Matthew and Luke were ignorant, as we are, of
what the missing leaf contained. From previous
indications in Mark we may infer that it told how
Jesus appeared in Galilee to Peter and the other
disciples, when he had risen from the dead.[17]

It is not in the Gospels, however, but in Paul's
First Epistle to the Corinthians that we have the
first and most authoritative account of the Resurrection.[18] Paul wrote it less than twenty-five years
after the event, and expressly says that his testimony is that of the immediate disciples themselves.
He declares that Jesus rose on the third day, and
appeared first to Peter, then to the twelve, then to
five hundred brethren at once, then to James, then
to all the Apostles. To these appearances he adds
that one which was vouchsafed to himself on the
way to Damascus. He says nothing of the scenes
at the tomb, and from the mention of "five hun-

---
[16] Mk. xvi. 8.
[17] Mk. xiv. 28; xvi. 7.
[18] I Cor. xv. 3–8.

FIRST AGE OF CHRISTIANITY 87

dred at once" we may conclude that the visions took place in Galilee, where the majority of Jesus' followers were still resident. It is significant that Paul speaks of his own vision of the risen Christ as the same in kind, though later in date than the others.

One fact emerges clearly from all the accounts, as well as from many other references in the New Testament—that the disciples fully believed that Jesus passed through death into a new life, and that they themselves had seen him. It is apparent, too, from the record of Paul that the evidence on which they relied was that of the appearances. On one occasion and another, under what conditions we are not told, the Lord whom they knew had stood before them in visual form. These appearances, so far as we can gather, all took place in Galilee, but later on they were assigned to Jerusalem, and were connected with the story of the empty tomb, which at the same time became more precise and elaborate. The narrative, as we now have it in its composite form, may have arisen in some such way as this. When the disciples returned to Galilee, Peter and after him the others had those wonderful experiences which convinced them that Jesus was still alive. Afterwards they met with the women who had stayed behind in Jerusalem to do the last honors to the dead, and who revealed to them what they had hitherto been afraid to mention, that they had found the tomb empty. This at first had only been accepted as confirmation of the visions, but in course of time it became the central fact in the whole narrative.

The disciples themselves, therefore, seem to have realized that the mere fact of the empty tomb could prove nothing. All emphasis in the earliest preaching was thrown on the visions. Many possibilities may be surmised which would sufficiently account for the empty tomb. The women in their confusion might have mistaken the place; or the body for some reason might have been removed, either by friends or enemies. Our belief in the Resurrection must rest on the positive fact that the disciples had some experience which convinced them that Jesus was still alive. For that part, the Resurrection ought not to be taken simply as a miraculous fact, standing by itself. Its whole significance lies in the divine life which led up to it and from which it cannot be separated. Jesus himself is the real proof of the Resurrection. The more we ponder our record of him, the more we realize the wonder of his personality, the more certain will it be to us that he died to live for ever. "He loosed the bonds of death," as Peter declared on the day of Pentecost, "because it was not possible that he should be holden of it." [19]

---

[19] Ac. ii. 24.

CHAPTER IV

THE TEACHING OF JESUS

(1) The Religious Basis

The life and the teaching of Jesus are interwoven in our Gospels, for neither of them can be understood without the other. In the light of the teaching we can discern the aims and motives which shaped the life; while the life explains many things that are obscure in the teaching. Jesus belonged to the ancient world and often employed terms and conceptions which have become strange to us, but his meaning is clear when we turn from his words to his example. It is the life, too, which gives power to the recorded words. An attempt has often been made to set forth the message of Jesus by means of typical sayings selected from the Gospels. These sayings do, in a manner, gather up the substance of what he taught, but every one can feel that when they are presented in abstract form the vital principle is wanting. The words of Jesus make their unique appeal to us because *he* spoke them. They do not stand by themselves but have behind them the convincing power of his personality and life.

It is here that we find the true answer to the

question so often asked as to the originality of his teaching. Men were conscious from the first that he had brought a new revelation, but its newness is hard to define. In his ethical conceptions he was at one, for the most part, with the Old Testament prophets. In his ideas of the future he took over many of the apocalyptic beliefs of his own day. For almost all of his sayings some parallel, more or less real, can be discovered in the rabbinical tradition. There are scholars who have concluded that he gave nothing that was distinctively new, but only repeated, in a more attractive form, the higher teaching of Judaism, liberating it at the same time from all that was merely local and temporary. It may indeed be granted that he borrowed from earlier teachers, as a builder makes use of materials which lie ready to his hand. His originality consisted in the new meaning he impressed on everything he borrowed, and in the never-failing insight with which he pierced through all externals to the inner truth. It consisted above all in the quickening power which he breathed out of his own spirit into all he taught. This is recognised by the fourth evangelist when he describes Jesus in his own Person as the Life and the Light. He himself, in the last resort, was the revelation.

It will be necessary at a later stage to examine this conception which is so wonderfully unfolded in the Fourth Gospel. In some respects the central purport of the message can be better understood from that Gospel than from any other record. The evangelist is a man of profound spiritual vis-

FIRST AGE OF CHRISTIANITY 91

ion who interprets the mind of Jesus in all the light that had been thrown on it by a century of Christian thought and experience. But for this purpose he often breaks away from the literal history. His concern is not so much with what Jesus actually said as with what he intended, when his words are taken in their ultimate purport. For our knowledge of the teaching as Jesus himself proclaimed it we must rely on the Synoptic Gospels.

We find, then, as we study these Gospels, that the message all turns on the idea of the Kingdom of God. Jesus came forward to announce that the Kingdom was near, to reveal the conditions on which men might enter it, to declare the nature of its new righteousness. In the later part of his ministry he claimed to be the Messiah through whom the Kingdom would come in, and finally died in the fulfilment of this great calling. What did he mean by the Kingdom, or, to render the word more exactly, the Kingship or Reign of God?

For the origin of the conception we must go back to the Old Testament. The prophets think of God as the supreme King, and foretell a time when He will destroy all hostile powers and assert His sole sovereignty. In the apocalyptic writings this idea of a coming reign of God had assumed a peculiar character. It was believed that the world's history would divide itself into two ages. During the first age, still in progress, the forces of evil had ruled unchecked; one heathen empire after another had usurped authority and had frustrated

God's purpose with the world. But there was a new age, soon to open, in which the present order would give place to another. A judgment would be held, in which the wicked would perish, and the people of God would be set apart for eternal life in a world from which all evil had disappeared. John the Baptist had taken up this hope of a coming Kingdom, and Jesus adopted it as the basis of his message. He taught that a crisis was at hand in which all the conditions of the world would become different, and that men must prepare themselves for this great change. They must live even now as if they belonged to the Kingdom, so that they might be ready for it when it arrived.

The idea of the Kingdom was thus a familiar one, and Jesus never deemed it necessary to explain it. He looked forward to a better age presently to set in. He took for granted that it would come about, not by any effort of man, but suddenly and miraculously by the act of God Himself. In two ways, however, he gave a new meaning to the traditional hope. (1) He discarded the pessimistic outlook on the world as it now is. For the apocalyptic thinkers the world was wholly evil. God had withdrawn for the time being from the government of the world, and would only interpose at some future day to dethrone the powers of evil. Jesus is confident that God is reigning now. His goodness is manifest in the rain and sunshine, in the wisdom with which all things are ordered, in the natural kindness of men to one another and the better impulses that keep rising in their hearts.

FIRST AGE OF CHRISTIANITY 93

When the Kingdom comes this presence of God will be fully apparent, but we can discern it already amidst all the darkness and confusion. (2) He thought of the Kingdom as a new moral order. The apocalyptists had been mainly intent on the changes that would come about in outward conditions. Disease and sorrow would disappear, the earth would yield more abundantly, all the limitations that cramp our present life would be removed. Jesus took little account of these external changes. His mind was wholly occupied with the spiritual conditions that would prevail when the old order had given place to the higher one. At present men are harsh and unjust to one another, they are ruled by false motives, they seek after earthly possessions and are blind to their true welfare. In the Kingdom they will obey the will of God, which is one of truth and righteousness. They will submit to it gladly and spontaneously, knowing that in God's service they have fulness of life. Thus we may say that while Jesus took over the apocalyptic hope it became for him a purely moral conception. The meaning which he gave to it is best expressed in the words of the Lord's Prayer—"Thy Kingdom come, thy will be done on earth as it is in heaven." For this reason it has a permanent value. In its literal form it belongs to a bygone age, and grew out of the peculiar history of the Jewish people. With our modern ideas we no longer expect a sudden cataclysm in which all things will be dissolved and a new world will miraculously emerge. Even within the New Testament period, as we shall see later, the church moved away from that literal conception of the Kingdom which meets us in the Gospels. But we still look forward to a time when right will prevail, when war and oppression will cease, when men will work together in a great brotherhood for noble ends. Life can have little meaning for us without this faith that the things which we know in our hearts to be highest will one day be triumphant. It was such a faith that possessed the mind of Jesus, and gave a lasting significance to his message of the Kingdom.

We must distinguish, therefore, between his essential thought and the form in which he expressed it. Taking up the apocalyptic hope which had long been current among pious Jews, he declared that the Kingdom was at hand. Everything that belonged to the old order was presently to lose its value, and men must prepare themselves to meet the new conditions. This they could only do in one way. Since the will of God would be the sole law of the Kingdom they must learn what it required, and conform their lives to its behests. The task which Jesus undertook was to reveal this will of God. Those who had gone before him had known God imperfectly, by the light of an uncertain tradition. He was himself conscious of a fellowship with God which was altogether new and by virtue of which he had an immediate insight into the divine mind and purpose.

This knowledge of God to which he laid claim was not of any mystical or speculative kind. He

FIRST AGE OF CHRISTIANITY 95

offered no proof of the existence of God, and does not seem to have conceived that any one could ever doubt it. He nowhere touches on the questions which at various times have perplexed philosophical thinkers; *e.g.* In what sense is God a Person? Is He immanent in the world or separate from it? How does He differ in essence from finite beings? Such questions, if he ever thought about them, seemed to him of little importance, and he was content with the old prophetic idea of God as the invisible Creator and Governor of the world, who has made man in His own image. His one interest is in the moral nature of God. The prophets had declared that He is the righteous God, and this idea is also fundamental for Jesus; but he sought to define for himself more clearly this divine righteousness. It is something more than an unerring justice which takes account of our doings and follows them with the due recompense. God's purpose towards us is one of mercy. He freely bestows on us the best gifts, and pardons us when we turn to Him, and unfailingly seeks our welfare. Jesus summed up this conception of God in the name "Father," or "heavenly Father." The name, it has often been pointed out in recent years, did not originate with him. There are passages in the Old Testament where it is plainly suggested.[1] In Jewish prayers of the time it was customary to address God as "our Father." What was original with Jesus was not the name but the full realisation of all that was involved in the name. There

---
[1] Cf. Ps. ciii. 13; Isai. lxiii. 16.

were many who had attained to the conviction that God was merciful, and that men could approach Him by right of a spiritual kinship. These beliefs find utterance in heathen as well as in Jewish piety; no religion is possible without some trace of them. The very idea of worship implies a feeling that we are somehow related to God, and that we can appeal from his strict justice to his compassion. But Jesus was the first to perceive the full consequences of this belief in God's Fatherhood. He realised that the love of God cannot be conceived merely as one attribute out of many. If God is loving, love must be central in his nature. He is our Father in the sense that all his purposes towards us are controlled by his infinite mercy. The name of "Father," as Jesus used it, was the symbol of a new conception of God, the boldest and grandest that has ever been.

It likewise involved a new conception of our relation to God. Since He is our Father, our attitude toward Him must be one of absolute trust. We can feel assured that our lives are precious to Him, and that we shall find our highest good in His service. For Jewish religion man's duty to God was summed up in the word "obedience," and this idea was primary also in the mind of Jesus. But in two ways he transformed the old conception. (1) He made little of the purely ritual service which counted for so much in all ancient religions. The obedience which God requires is not a formal one, limited to certain outward ceremonies, but must embrace the whole life. Our thoughts and

FIRST AGE OF CHRISTIANITY 97

desires, as well as our actions, must be conformed to God's will. (2) He declared that obedience must be free and spontaneous, and otherwise means nothing. For the Pharisees the will of God was something imposed from without, in the prescriptions of a written code. They made it their aim to do exactly what the Law demanded, no less and no more. Jesus insisted that there must be no measure to our obedience. We are to make the will of God our own will, so that we act on it always, by an inward impulse, almost without our knowing. Here we can discern the purpose which underlies the whole teaching of Jesus. It can best be stated in his own words, "that ye may be the children of your Father who is in heaven."[2] Other teachers, before and since, have defined man's task as that of realizing, ever more fully, his kinship with the divine nature. The Greek thinkers, for instance, conceived of God as the infinite Reason, and taught that men could become like God by cultivating the reason He had given them. Jesus set out from a different conception of God's nature. He thought of Him as the Father, who is altogether good and just and holy. We become His children, we enter into fellowship with Him, not by any mystical or intellectual process but by growing more like Him in our moral nature. Again and again, in varying language, Jesus maintains that those who know God best are those who do His will, with a perfect simplicity of heart. Since the very being of God is absolute goodness

[2] Mt. v. 35.

(2) THE ETHICAL TEACHING

we can only attain to Him when we act in our narrow sphere as He does in his universe.

It is for this reason that the teaching of Jesus consists for the most part of moral precepts. Many people have risen from their study of the Gospels with a secret disappointment. They have expected light on the ultimate mysteries, and have seemed to find nothing but homely counsels on duty to one's neighbour and the ways of right living. Attempts have been made, from the first century onwards, to convert this plain teaching into some abstruse metaphysical doctrine. This, however, is to miss the profound idea which lies at the heart of it. Believing as he did that the essential nature of God was active love and goodness, Jesus sought to impress on us the tremendous import of the moral life. By doing God's will in the common tasks and duties we have fellowship with God, and there is no other way. This deeper intention has always to be borne in mind as we study the Gospel sayings. It is true that all the stress is laid on practical goodness, and from this it has often been inferred that the whole object of Jesus was ethical. We are told that men can adopt the Sermon on the Mount as their rule of conduct even though they separate it altogether from any religious belief. But the teaching of Jesus is rooted in religion, and apart from it has no meaning. He held that the one aim of life is to become children of the heavenly Father. He thought of the moral duties as the means appointed whereby we may attain to this likeness to God. We share in His nature, we become one with Him, according as we realize His will in our common life.

From this it follows that right action, as Jesus conceives it, must proceed from a right disposition. His purpose all through his teaching is to change and renew the will, so that the thoughts and deeds will grow out of it like good fruit out of a good tree.[8] It might appear at first sight as though he lays down a great number of separate commands, bearing on one aspect and another of human life and duty. Fifty years after his death he had come to be regarded as a lawgiver, similar to Moses but greater, who had drawn up the final code for right living. This idea has persisted in various forms ever since. It has been assumed that he set himself to legislate for man's conduct in all the relations of life, and the complaint is often made that his teaching is defective on one side and another. When he is viewed as a moralist or law-giver this complaint is just. There were many questions already urgent in his own day on which he said nothing. Problems of the first magnitude have since emerged which lay quite outside of his horizon. His precepts cannot be adopted as a complete system of rules by which we may guide our action in all the moral perplexities of our modern world. But he never professed to offer such a system. The very thing against which he protested was the effort to regulate all conduct by definite

---
[8] Mt. vii. 16; Lk. vi. 43.

rules. This effort had been made in the legal religion of his time, and had resulted in the lifeless, conventional morality of the scribes and Pharisees. Instead of rules Jesus laid down a few great principles, and required that men should think them out, and decide for themselves, on each occasion, how they should be applied. His separate sayings and parables, when we come to examine them, are nothing but illustrations of those vital principles. And behind all else there is the demand for a right will. All that matters, in the last resort, is the inward disposition out of which our life proceeds. If the will is false the most exemplary behavior is nothing but hypocrisy. When the will has been renewed no rules or injunctions are any longer necessary, and a man may safely be left to direct his own action as he sees best. The great object of Jesus was to effect this renewal of the will. When John the Baptist had called for repentance he had nothing in mind but a visible change of conduct. The dishonest or violent man was to turn over a new leaf; the avaricious man was to relieve the needs of others.[4] Jesus demanded a radical change of nature. "Unless ye turn and become like little children ye cannot enter the Kingdom of God."[5]

Jesus has been regarded as a legislator for the moral life, and sometimes it has been held that his main interest was that of the social reformer. Most of his sayings are concerned with the duties we owe to our neighbours. His whole teaching cen-

[4] Lk. iii. 10 ff.
[5] Mt. xviii. 3.

FIRST AGE OF CHRISTIANITY

tres on the idea of the coming Kingdom, when men will form one brotherhood in the service of God. Ever since the church began, and not least in our own day, stress has been laid on the social aspects of his message. It has been assumed that he wished to reorganize society and that he put forward some definite scheme for this purpose. Again and again his name has been appealed to on one side or another of political controversy. Now it is true that he indicated the broad principles on which social righteousness must always be founded. He taught that all are brethren and owe a duty to one another, most of all to the weak and poor and suffering who have most need of their help. He insisted that every human personality has a value of its own in the sight of God, and that no man must be exploited for the greed or pleasure of his fellow man. These principles and others like them are capable of an infinite application. They strike at the root of all forms of society which involve unjust privilege or purely material ideals. The effort to give ever larger effect to them has been the mainspring of all progress during the Christian centuries. But social reform was not the primary aim of Jesus. The great fact for him was not the community but the human soul, with its capacity for a higher life, in fellowship with God. He recognized, however, as none had done before him, that this life can only be developed through the social relations. It is in intercourse with our fellow men that we can exercise those qualities which make us akin to God

—love, pity, forgiveness, self-sacrifice. The more we spend ourselves for our neighbours the more we attain to our own true life. This, it may be said, is the paradox that runs all through the teaching of Jesus. The supreme task for every man is to enter for himself into the Kingdom of God, yet he can only accomplish this task by utterly forgetting himself in service to others. It is Jesus' chief criticism of the Pharisees that their good actions are all done for themselves, with the deliberate aim of winning favour from God. The true disciple must be unconscious of self. His right hand must not know what the left is doing. "He that saveth his life shall lose it, and he that loseth his life the same shall find it."[6]

(3) The Messianic Claim

Jesus availed himself, then, of the Jewish apocalyptic ideas in order to convey a religious message of inexhaustible value. He contrasted the present age with one that is coming, when the will of God will be the sole law. He called on men to prepare themselves for that new age by following God's will even now, and made clear to them what it consisted in. God is righteous and holy, his nature is one of infinite love and goodness. The great end of men must be to act as He does. They must enter into such fellowship with Him that His will takes possession of them, and directs them at all times as if it were their own. This fellowship is made possible by complete trust in God.[7] Be-

---
[6] Mt. xvi. 25; Lk. ix. 24.
[7] Mt. vi. 25 ff.

FIRST AGE OF CHRISTIANITY 103

lieving in Him as our Father we can yield ourselves to Him without reserve; all else will follow from this act of faith, of absolute surrender to God. It was therefore the grand aim of Jesus to inspire in men that perfect confidence in God which is the secret of true life. By word and parable he taught them to think of God as he himself did. He spoke of God's forgiveness, of his love and wisdom, of his watchful care for even the least of his creatures. It was by his own personality, however, that he chiefly impressed on men his new conception of God. This was realized even in his own lifetime. The whole Gospel story illustrates the manner in which he awakened in those who met him a new sense of God. By their knowledge of himself he enabled them to believe in God's love and mercy. He was himself aware that he possessed this power. It is doubtful whether he spoke the actual words attributed to him by Matthew and Luke, "No man hath known the Son but the Father, neither hath any man known the Father save the Son."[a] Yet these words sum up the conviction which certainly underlay all his work. He came forward as one who could lead men to God, who was himself in such a relation to God that he could make Him manifest to others. He was conscious of a commission by right of which he could perform miracles and forgive sins. It is this sense of a unique authority which gives significance to all his words and deeds.

---
[a] Mt. xi. 27; Lk. x. 22.

From this point of view we must interpret his teaching on his Messiahship. Assured that he had a relation to God such as no other had, he could not but express this conviction in terms of those apocalyptic ideas which determined his message of the kingdom. According to prophecy the Kingdom was to come about through the Messiah, who would appear as God's representative, and Jesus declared that he was this promised Messiah. There is evidence, as we have seen, that he arrived at this belief gradually and reluctantly. Not only did he shrink from the tremendous responsibility which the claim involved, but he was sensible of its inadequacy. Bound up as it was with the national hopes of Israel, the Messianic idea did not fully correspond with the aim he had set before him. Some modern scholars have held that he himself never made the claim, and that it was only put forward on his behalf by his disciples after his death. But this view is utterly unwarranted. It is not too much to say that if the Gospels had made no mention of Jesus' claim to be Messiah we should have had to assume it in order to make the story intelligible. We cannot explain his sense of authority, the devotion of his followers, the fears of his enemies, the circumstances of his death, the emergence of the Christian Church, on any other ground than that he declared himself the Messiah.

It is probable, at the same time, that he thought of this supreme dignity as of one that would be conferred on him in the future. The Messiah is described in the apocalyptic books as a heavenly being who will suddenly appear in clouds of glory to inaugurate the new age. Jesus was a man on earth, beset with earthly suffering and limitation. But he looked to a day when he would be manifested in a new character. Through death he would rise to his Messiahship and would return from heaven to fulfil his destined work. That this was his expectation is probable from the strange title, "Son of man," by which he designated himself in the closing period of his ministry. There can be little doubt that it goes back to the passage in Daniel which tells how the seer in a vision beheld "one like a Son of man" approach the throne of God and receive from Him an everlasting kingdom.[9] In this mysterious passage the "Son of man" appears to be Israel, typified as a human figure in contrast with the brute-like, heathen empires which had gone before. But the name had been transferred by later apocalyptic writers to the Messiah in his character as a heavenly being. From Matthew and Luke we should gather that Jesus habitually spoke of himself by this name, but Mark makes it clear that he only used it sparingly, and in a special context. As Son of man he would appear hereafter in glory to judge the world and bring in the Kingdom of God.[10]

To this rule, however, there is one striking exception. The title which marks out his future ex-

[9] Dan. vii. 13, 14.
[10] Mk. xiii. 26; xiv. 62.

altation is also associated with his coming death at the hands of his enemies. "The Son of man shall be delivered to the chief priests and scribes and they shall condemn him to death and deliver him to the Gentiles" (Mk. x. 33). A number of problems arise out of this singular use of the lofty title, but one thing seems clear. The sense of his Messiahship was closely connected in the mind of Jesus with the anticipation of his death. He was confident that the death, which to the eyes of men would mean the ruin of his work, was the means appointed by God for its fulfilment. Not merely in spite of the seeming disaster but somehow because of it, would he be exalted to his place as Messiah. That he related his glory to his suffering is borne out by all his utterances on the Messianic claim. He never speaks of it without some allusion to the necessity of his death. The two convictions that he was the promised Messiah and that he must die at the hands of his enemies grew up in his mind together. In earlier thought the Messiah was always conceived as a conqueror, who would accomplish his work almost without effort, by the mere "breath of his mouth." Jesus was ever conscious that the supreme dignity must involve the supreme suffering. However else we may explain this consciousness it was rooted in a profound instinct which reveals itself in some of the most impressive of his sayings. True greatness, he perceived, was inseparable from sacrifice. "He that would be first among you must be the servant of all."[11] The Messiah himself would not be exempt from this appointed law that suffering is the one path to sovereignty. "The Son of man came not to be ministered unto but to minister and to give his life a ransom for many."[12]

It has often been held that the later church made a radical departure from the intention of Jesus by putting his death at the centre of his gospel. The fact of his death seemed evidence that he had come into the world to die, and his message of the Kingdom was allowed to fall into the background, giving place entirely to the gospel of the Cross. In this manner, we are told, the real teaching of Jesus was obscured and distorted. But it may justly be answered that in placing the emphasis on the redeeming death the Apostles were true to the implications of Jesus' own thought. He believed that through his death, and not otherwise, he would attain to his destined place and accomplish his work. How he conceived that it would have this efficacy we cannot tell, and perhaps he never formed to himself anything like a reasoned doctrine. He was content to know that since God had clearly willed his death it was necessary that he should die. The Kingdom could not come in without this sacrifice.

However this may be we cannot doubt, as we survey the whole tenor of the life and teaching of Jesus, that everything leads up to the Cross and there finds its explanation. That ministry of love

---
[11] Lk. xxii. 26; Mk. ix. 35.
[12] Mk. x. 45

108 FIRST AGE OF CHRISTIANITY

and service and loyalty to the highest would have missed its crown if it had found any other end. Its grandest meanings would have remained hidden, and it would have lacked the divine power by which it has changed the world. Jesus had declared that God is our Father, that by fellowship with God we attain to life, that this fellowship consists in utter obedience to God's will. By his own death he summed up and drove home to the hearts of men the message he had proclaimd in words.

THE PRIMITIVE CHURCH

(1) THE SOURCES

For all our direct knowledge of the earliest history of the church we are indebted to the book of Acts, which forms the sequel to the Gospel of Luke. It is dedicated, like the Gospel, to Theophilus, an earnest and intelligent Gentile, who wished to be more fully instructed in the new religion.[1] According to a tradition which was never questioned until recent times the book of Acts, like the accompanying Gospel, was written by Luke, a physician who probably belonged to Antioch, and who is several times mentioned by Paul as one of his assistants. That a companion of Paul had some part in the writing of the book is evident from the use, in certain sections, of the pronoun "we," by which the author includes himself among the persons of the story.[2] These "we" sections are all concerned with the *travels* of Paul, and it is held by some modern scholars that Luke was only responsible for a travel-diary, which was worked up by a later writer into an extended history of the Apostolic times. But no sufficient reason for questioning

---
[1] Lk. i. 1-4; Ac. i. 1.
[2] Ac. xvi. 10-17; xx. 5-15; xxi. 1-18; xxvii. 1; xxviii. 16.

Luke's authorship of the whole work has yet been brought forward. In style and thought and vocabulary the "travel-diary" closely resembles the rest of the book, and appears to have come from the same hand.

Like the Gospel to which it is appended the book of Acts is a compilation. This is especially true of the first twelve chapters, which narrate the history of the church in those earlier years which lay outside of the writer's personal knowledge. It is clear that for this part of his work he had scanty information. He is able to record only a few incidents, strongly colored by legend, and even these he appears to tell twice over. The arrest of the Apostles, the sharing of goods in the primitive church, the trial and death of Stephen are all described in two versions which in substance repeat each other. From this it has been inferred that he obtained his data from two documents, one composed in Jerusalem and the other in Antioch, which he weaves together, much as he had combined Mark and Q in his Gospel. Certain peculiar turns in the language of this first half of the book make it highly probable that the documents were in Aramaic. For the life of Paul he would be able to draw on his own knowledge and on the reminiscences of friends who had accompanied the Apostle on his journeys. He seems also to have availed himself of a few written documents, of an official character, which had come into his hands.

The book of Acts is thus based on trustworthy records, and has a real historical value. This is impaired to some extent by motives and theories which have biassed the author in his presentation of the facts. (1) He holds that the Christian mission was promoted and supervised by the mother-church in Jerusalem, and adapts the history to this view. (2) He refuses to admit that there was any conflict among the early Apostles, although it is evident from the Epistles that Paul had to struggle all his life against a bitter opposition. (3) At the time he wrote the church had come under the suspicion of the Roman government; the age of persecution had begun. It is therefore one of his prime objects to show that in earlier days the mission had been regarded as politically harmless. Again and again complaints had been lodged against it, but these, when duly examined by Roman magistrates, had always been set aside. It can hardly be doubted that Luke has sometimes slurred over the facts or has even perverted them under the influence of this apologetic motive. Here, too, we have the best explanation of one of the problems of the book—its abrupt close just at the point when Paul is about to stand his trial before the supreme court at Rome. This trial and its sequel would form the natural climax of the story, but we are not allowed to reach it. The reason almost certainly is that after insisting on the uniform friendliness of Rome the author does not care to tell how it had finally condemned the foremost Apostle. (4) Luke is possessed of a strong dramatic instinct and a remarkable gift for vivid and interesting narrative. It is these qualities which make his work so fascinating, but they sometimes impair its historical value. He is led away by the temptation to tell an effective story, even when he cannot do so without departing from the strict facts.

The evidence of the book of Acts requires, whenever possible, to be carefully checked by that of Paul's Epistles. Paul does not pretend to be in any sense an historian. He writes to his churches as their guide and teacher, and his references to events are all incidental to his main purpose. But they have the value which always attaches to firsthand testimony. Luke was at best a secondary actor in the up-building of the church, and he wrote after the lapse of a generation when his memories were partly dimmed. Paul was himself the chief of the Apostles. In his matchless letters he gives us his impression of events while they were still in process of happening. It is now recognized that in any attempt to trace the history of the primitive church we must take our departure from the statements and allusions of Paul. By themselves they are fragmentary, and without the light afforded by the book of Acts we should not be able to estimate their true bearing. Without Acts, too, we should not be able to place the facts, as we know them them from Paul's Epistles, in their right chronological order. Luke is our historian, and with all his shortcomings we owe him an incalculable debt; but the value of his record is immensely enhanced because we can supplement and correct it by the direct evidence of Paul.

FIRST AGE OF CHRISTIANITY

(2) The Beginning of the Church

Jesus in his lifetime had not tried to form any organization for the carrying on of his work. He had taught that religion consists not in outward rules and arrangements but in a right will, an inward service of God. More than once he speaks of all institutions as belonging to the present imperfect order. In the new age, when the will of God is the sole law, they will be necessary no longer.

It is true that he gathered around him a body of followers, probably much larger than is commonly supposed. Besides the twelve disciples who were his personal disciples an ever-increasing number of men and women had been led to acknowledge him as their leader. Paul speaks of "more than five hundred at once" to whom he appeared after his Resurrection,[3] and these would be only the enthusiasts among a much larger following. But these men and women who had been attracted to the new teaching do not seem to have been bound together in any formal union. Jesus had himself declared that the one bond among his disciples was to be a common spirit of love and service.[4] When he was asked to assign ranks and offices he had deliberately refused.

Within a few years after his death this brotherhood of believers had become a great organization. The "church" had come into being and had taken

---
[3] I Cor. xv. 6.
[4] Lk. xxii. 24, 25; Mk. x. 35–45.

the first steps in the development which was to make it the mightiest institution that has ever been. How this had come about we cannot tell. The author of the book of Acts can only offer us a few meagre hints, and probably the true facts were never known even to the chief actors. The new movement, it must never be forgotten, was launched on a great wave of enthusiasm. Men were not fully conscious of what they were doing. They were urged on by forces which they could not control, and of which they could render no account. Before they clearly perceived that anything had happened the church had taken definite shape.

From Acts we can gather that after the Resurrection appearances a body of Jesus' followers, about one hundred and twenty in all, made their way to Jerusalem.[5] They came there most likely in the confidence that their Master was to return almost immediately as the triumphant Messiah, and would suddenly appear, as prophecy had foretold, in the temple.[6] The first act of this devoted company was to appoint one of their number to take the place of the traitor Judas. The choice was made by lot, and fell on one Matthias, of whom nothing further is known. Since the return of Jesus was expected at any hour his followers seem at first to have attempted no mission, but spent their time in eager waiting, either in the courts of the temple or in some upper room where they prayed and conversed together. The practice be-

[5] Ac. i. 15.
[6] Malachi iii. 1.

FIRST AGE OF CHRISTIANITY 115

gan at this time of repeating, at the close of a common meal, the rite of breaking of bread which Jesus had observed at the Last Supper. By thus recalling his pledge the disciples confirmed themselves in their hope that he would presently return. Those earliest believers were probably all Galilaeans, who had given up their occupations and settled in the strange city without any means of livelihood. Whatever they possessed they threw into a common stock, and were thus able to satisfy their simple needs. Convinced as they were that the time was all but come when earthly possessions would be useless, they shared all things without grudging.

From the first the leading place was taken by Peter. Not only had he been the foremost disciple in Jesus's lifetime, and the first witness of the Resurrection, but his character was such as to make him the natural head of an enthusiastic movement. As we know him alike from the Gospels and the later history he was a man of warm and generous nature, capable of a passionate loyalty. At a subsequent time, when gifts of intellect and governing power were needed, Peter fell into a secondary place, but in those first days the one thing necessary was the glowing faith which could kindle the faith of others, and Peter had this in the highest measure. Without him the church could hardly have survived the first critical days.

The real beginning of the church, according to Acts, was on the day of Pentecost, seven weeks after the Crucifixion. On that day the believers were met together, after their custom, when a sudden impulse came upon them and they "spoke with tongues." Assured by this sign that they had received the Spirit from heaven they went out among the people and began to proclaim their message. There is much that is puzzling in the story, but we can hardly doubt that it preserves the memory of an all-important event. In the years that followed everything was to turn on the conviction that a supernatural power had been bestowed on the church. It was this confidence that they possessed the Spirit, promised to God's people in the new age, which enabled the disciples to rise above themselves and work for the cause of Christ with a boundless courage and devotion. They seem first to have become aware of this divine power in that meeting on the day of Pentecost, when they began to "speak with tongues." We know from Paul's discussion of it in I Cor. xii.–xiv., that this continued to be a common phenomenon in Christian worship, and that it consisted in the outpouring of inarticulate sounds, under the stress of an overmastering emotion. The phenomenon is one to which many parallels can be found in the history of religious revivals down to our own day. Sometimes in these later instances the meaningless sounds have been so diversified as to bear all the appearance of a language, and efforts have been made to identify it. Paul is convinced that the language represented in the tongues was no other than that of heaven. The "tongues of angels" are contrasted with "the tongues of men."[7] The author of Acts

---
[7] I Cor. xiii. 1.

appears to hold the theory that actual earthly languages were spoken on the day of Pentecost, and were intelligible to many of the strangers who had come up for the feast. In that first proclamation of the gospel in foreign tongues he sees a symbol and forecast of its coming diffusion over all the world.

With the day of Pentecost the Christian mission began. The disciples, inspired as they now believed by a power from above, were no longer content to wait passively for the Lord's coming. They fervidly proclaimed their hope in Jerusalem itself and in the neighbouring towns and villages, and the number of believers rapidly increased. It might seem strange that in face of this growing movement the religious authorities, who had set themselves so implacably against Jesus, did not interfere. Once or twice, we are told, the leading Apostles were called before the Council, but were released almost at once with a mild admonition. This immunity granted to the church in the earliest days, when it might have been crushed so easily, is doubtless to be explained from the loyalty of the disciples to the Law. Judaism has always allowed a wide latitude to opinions. On condition that a man holds fast to the legal observances it does not meddle with his beliefs. The disciples, it was clear, had no intention of transgressing the Law. They practiced it even more rigorously than other pious Jews, and the authorities had no choice but to leave them alone. At a later time their fidelity to the Law was to prove the chief hindrance to the progress of

Christianity, but it is only fair to remember that in the first days it served a great purpose. If the church had set out with the attitude which Paul was to take later it would certainly have been strangled in the cradle.

The members of the community were not yet known by any distinctive name. They called themselves the "brethren," the "believers," the "disciples," "those who waited for the coming of Jesus Christ." So far from suspecting that they were the pioneers of a new religion they tried in every possible way to mark their adherence to Judaism, of which they claimed to be the true representatives. Ever since the time of the Prophets a distinction had been made between the mass of the nation and the "remnant"—the small minority of faithful souls who were "Israelites indeed"—true to the ideal vocation of Israel. The followers of Jesus claimed to be this elect "remnant," and this was probably the origin of the name "the Ecclesia" or "church." In the Greek translation of the Old Testament the name is applied to Israel as the community of God's people. It served to designate the disciples as the nucleus of that true Israel in which the promises of God would at last be fulfilled.

But while the church was thus nothing in appearance but a Jewish sect it was distinguished from the first by certain customs and beliefs which contained in them the germ of the whole later development. In its worship it practised the rite of baptism, taken over from John the Baptist, and its own special rite of the Lord's Supper. It gave a place, moreover, to those ecstatic outbreaks of which the speaking with tongues was the most remarkable, and which were supposed to be due to the operation of the Spirit. In its social life it tried to give practical effect to the precepts of Jesus. The men and women who composed it formed an association which corresponded on a larger scale with Jesus' company of disciples. They were "brethren," all on a footing of equality in the service of a common Master. Above all, while it held the ordinary beliefs of Judaism the church was marked out by certain new convictions which determined all its thought and worship. It believed that the promised Messiah had now appeared in Jesus of Nazareth, that he had risen from the dead and was still in fellowship with his people, that he would shortly come again and bring in the Kingdom of God.

From the outset the movement seems to have found a notable response among the Hellenists, or Greek-speaking Jews. For more than a century past large numbers of Jews had settled, chiefly for purposes of commerce, in foreign cities, and many of them had found their way back to Jerusalem. These returned exiles were usually men of an earnest religious spirit, anxious to end their days in the holy city, under the shadow of the temple. It is not difficult to guess why they, more than others, were attracted to the new teaching. By their contact with a larger world their outlook had been broadened, more than they were aware, and when they came back to Jerusalem they were apt to be

120 FIRST AGE OF CHRISTIANITY

bitterly disillusioned. Instead of the religious ardor they had dreamed of they too often found nothing but the wranglings of worldly priests and the endless hair-splitting of the interpreters of the Law. In the Chrisian community they breathed a larger and more spiritual atmosphere. Here was Judaism at its best, set free from all that narrowed and perverted it. Here, if anywhere, was the real feeling for religion. We cannot wonder that in a short time the Hellenists formed a considerable portion of the church, and their advent was to have all-important consequences.

The first grave crisis in the history was directly due to the presence of this foreign element. With its increasing numbers the community found it more and more difficult to maintain the principle that all things were to be held in common. Complaints arose that some were receiving more than others, and the Hellenists, perhaps on good grounds, felt that they were being treated as outsiders. It was finally decided that two sections should be formed within the brotherhood. The older Apostles were to devote themselves wholly to the native Jews, while seven men were appointed to take special charge of the aliens.[8] From the account in Acts it might appear as if the difference arose wholly on the question of practical administration, but there are signs that this only brought it to a head. It is significant that of the seven men elected, Stephen and Philip at once came forward as active missionaries. The Hellenists had discovered that their own

---
[8] Ac. vi. 1–6.

FIRST AGE OF CHRISTIANITY 121

view of the Gospel was not entirely that of their Palestinian brethren, and they wanted Apostles who would represent it. They won their case, and Stephen, one of the new teachers, immediately became prominent. From the little that is told us it seems clear that he was the most remarkable man who had yet appeared in the church. He was gifted and eloquent and full of ardor, and if he had lived would doubtless have ranked among the very greatest of the Apostles. As it was his career can hardly have lasted more than a few months or weeks. His teaching in the Hellenistic synagogues made it apparent for the first time that the new movement involved a danger to the Law, and an outcry arose against him. He was brought before the council on a charge of blasphemy, and the feeling against him was so strong that he was dragged out and stoned to death while the trial was still in process. That Saul of Tarsus had a part in the accusation of Stephen is more than likely, but there is no evidence that he was responsible for his death. Stephen was not condemned and executed at the instance of Saul. The council had no power to pass a death sentence, and in any case it was not allowed to bring the trial to a finish. Stephen was killed by an angry mob which took the law into its own hands.

His death, though it was not brought about in any deliberate manner, was an event of crucial importance. Hitherto the church had been left unmolested, but now the authorities took measures against it. They distinguished, however, between the two sections, showing that the cleavage was already so pronounced that the outside world was fully aware of it. Peter and the native Christians were allowed to remain in the city, while the followers of Stephen were driven in all directions.[9] Some of them no doubt returned to their old homes in Rome and Alexandria, and became the founders of the famous churches in these great capitals. Others made their way to Damascus and Antioch, the nearest large cities beyond the bounds of Palestine. At Antioch they proceeded at once to carry out a vigorous mission among the Jewish population, but soon, and almost by accident, the work assumed a larger scope.[10] In the great cosmopolitan city there were many who had become interested in Judaism, and these Gentile proselytes were strongly drawn to the new teaching. Antioch became the cradle of the Gentile mission, and at Antioch, too, the Christians first received the name which they were henceforth to bear.[11] Why was this name of Latin formation bestowed on them in a Greek-speaking city? Most probably it was modelled on the partisan names which had become familiar everywhere during the civil wars, (Sullani, Caesariani, Pompeiani). It was thus given by way of malice or derision to mark the followers of a new pretender to empire. For almost a century the Christians themselves refused to accept the name.

The Gentile mission, therefore, was not deliber-

---

[9] Ac. viii. 1.
[10] Ac. xi. 19, 20.
[11] Ac. xi. 26.

ately planned, but neither was it the result of mere accident. It came about, rather, from the very nature of the new message. Jesus had been born a Jew and had taught under Jewish forms of thought, but his gospel had nothing to do with any racial peculiarities. It was a universal gospel, and sooner or later even though the history had taken a quite different turn, was bound to find its way out of the confines of Judaism and appeal to the world at large. For a long time after the Gentile mission had become a mighty fact the original disciples looked on it with misgiving and did their best to hinder it. In spite of everything Christianity grew into a world-religion by the sheer force of its universal character.

(3) THE CONVERSION OF PAUL

While the Gentile mission was struggling into existence at Antioch, the man who was destined to be its champion had come into the church. Saul was a native of Tarsus in Cilicia, but his family, though settled in a Greek city, was of pure Jewish descent and strongly attached to the Law. His father, probably for some notable service to one of the armies during the civil wars, had received the coveted honor of Roman citizenship; and in addition to his Jewish name Saul bore the Roman one of Paul. From childhood he must have shown a religious and intellectual bent, for he was destined to the office of a Rabbi, although, in accordance with an excellent Jewish custom, he also learned a handicraft, that of tent-making, or perhaps more accurately, of weaving tent-ropes from the goat's hair (cilicium) for which his native province was famous. Following up his studies as a Rabbi he eventually came to Jerusalem, just at the time when the Christian teaching had become notorious. Some have inferred from his enigmatic words in II Cor. v. 16 ("though we have known Christ after the flesh yet now we know him so no more") that he must have been present in the city during the fatal Passover week, but this is unlikely. If he had ever had personal acquaintance with Jesus, however slight, he could not have failed to insist on it, in view of the oft-repeated charge against him that he was not an immediate disciple. His arrival must have taken place at some time between the Crucifixion and the brief career of Stephen. When the council took measures against Stephen's followers after his death Paul threw himself ardently into the work of repression. Perhaps at his own request he was sent to Damascus to excite the local synagogue against the fugitives. The synagogue in this city, which lay outside of the jurisdiction of the council, would have very limited powers. The worst penalty it could inflict would be that of excommunicating its own refractory members. Paul was no doubt at this time bitterly opposed to the Christian movement, but he never had the opportunity of being the blood-thirsty persecutor which later tradition made him.

On the way to Damascus the event took place which suddenly changed him from an enemy of the new faith into its foremost Apostle. In his own

FIRST AGE OF CHRISTIANITY 125

Epistles, Paul makes four references to his conversion (Gal. i. 13-16; I Cor. ix. 1; II Cor. iv. 6; I Cor. xv. 8), and in the book of Acts we have three accounts of it, but they are so much at variance, and so coloured with fanciful details that we cannot determine the precise facts.[12] It appears certain, however, alike from the narratives in Acts and from Paul's own references, that he saw a radiance which he believed to be Jesus, appearing to him in his risen and glorified body. He was convinced, then and afterwards, that the vision had an objective reality, but at the same time he thought of it as an inward revelation (Gal. i.16 "to reveal his Son in me"). He had "seen Jesus" as truly as the first disciples had done; he had also had the first of those mystical experiences in which he held communion with the indwelling Christ. Modern psychology would lay stress on the subconscious process which must have led up to the great moment of the conversion. Paul had listened to Stephen and perhaps had seen him die, looking to heaven "with his face like that of an angel." He had been moved far more than he knew by the Christian message, and the very hatred which it aroused in him was a sign that he was strangely attracted to it, in spite of himself. His mind had been working towards a crisis which was suddenly precipitated by something that happened on the way to Damascus. But at this point all is mystery, which is not in any way dispelled by so-called psychological explanations. We only know that at

---

[12] Ac. ix. 3–7; xxii. 4–11; xxvi. 12–19.

the decisive moment there broke in on the mind of Paul a great conviction which transformed his life.

He proceeded to Damascus, where he immediately joined himself to the Christian community and was baptized. But after the great upheaval he felt the need of an interval of solitude and retired into "Arabia," the desert region which lay to the east.[13] Returning to the city he entered on his work as a Christian missionary. For the best part of three years he remained in Damascus, and by his energy in the Christian cause drew on himself the bitter hostility of the Jewish population, which sought, with the help of the local authorities, to put him to death. The gates of the city were guarded to prevent his escape, but in the darkness he was let down from the walls by a rope, and made for Jerusalem, which he had not visited since his conversion.[14] Even now he only stayed a fortnight in the city, and kept himself all the time in seclusion. His chief object in this visit was to make the acquaintance of Peter. We should give much to know something of the conversation which went on during those days between the two men.

(4) THE COUNCIL OF JERUSALEM

It is clear that Paul had already resolved to devote himself to work in the Gentile countries. After his brief sojourn in Jerusalem he went to Tarsus, his native city, and shortly afterwards was summoned by Barnabas, whose friendship he had al-

---
[13] Gal. i. 17.
[14] Ac. ix. 23 ff; II Cor. xi. 32, 33.

FIRST AGE OF CHRISTIANITY 127

ready made, to assist him in the mission at Antioch. Here he continued to labour for fourteen years. Nothing is known in detail of his life during this long period, but we cannot understand his later career unless we bear in mind those formative years at Antioch. In this great city, the third largest in the Roman empire, he was thrown in contact with men of all nationalities. He grew aware of the world's need for Christianity, and learned how the Christian teaching could be so presented as to appeal to every race. The idea gradually arose in his mind of a mission which should make the whole world acquainted with the gospel.

At last in company with Barnabas and with the full sanction of the church at Antioch, he set out on what is commonly known as the first missionary journey. This division of his missionary life into three journeys is convenient but somewhat misleading. We are rather to think of his work as falling into two great periods, in the first of which he had Antioch as his headquarters, while in the second he broke away from Antioch and made use of different bases in Asia Minor and Europe. The so-called first journey was little more than a preliminary survey of the field. From Antioch the Apostles crossed to the neighbouring island of Cyprus, and after traversing it from end to end passed over to the southern coast of Asia Minor. They made short stays in the larger cities—Perga, Antioch in Pisidia, Iconium, Lystra, Derbe—and then, returning by the same route, sailed home to Antioch. For some time it appeared as if the enterprise were to meet with little success, and Mark, the youthful nephew of Barnabas, whom the two Apostles had taken with them as their companion, lost heart at an early stage and left them. But at Antioch in Pisidia they received a cordial welcome, which was repeated in the other cities. As a result of their journey they left behind them a number of small but vigorous communities, and were fully satisfied that a great field was open in the Gentile world for the proclamation of the gospel.

Until this time Gentiles had been admitted into the church as a matter of favor. It was taken for granted that the gospel was primarily for the Jews, and aliens who put their faith in Christ were also expected to observe the Jewish law. Paul had felt that this was unnecessary. The great truth had dawned on him that Christianity was not a mere phase of Judaism but a new religion, grounded on faith instead of on legal obedience. In his work at Antioch he had ventured to accept Gentile converts on the condition of faith alone. Visitors from Jerusalem had protested against this innovation, and the controversy came to a head shortly after Paul's return from his first journey. He saw that the time had come for obtaining a clear decision on this vital question. Along with Barnabas he went up to Jerusalem to confer with the leading Apostles, taking with him Titus, a young convert of great promise who had not undergone the Jewish rite of circumcision. Titus was to be the test case. Was a Gentile who manifestly had the true faith in

FIRST AGE OF CHRISTIANITY 129

Christ to be rejected because he had not first become a Jew?

This Council of Jerusalem (49 A. D.) marks the chief turning-point in the history of the early church. About seventeen years had now passed since the death of Stephen, and all this time the church at Jerusalem had been growing more Jewish in character. If the Hellenists had been permitted to remain they would gradually have leavened the community and the later struggle might not have been necessary. But while they dispersed among the foreign cities to maintain and develop their freer gospel the mother-church had become more conservative. It was now dominated by a man of very different character from Peter, who with all his weaknesses had a broad and liberal spirit. James, who had taken his place, was distinguished even among the Jews for his rigid observance of the Law. He was clearly an able man, of strong personality, but his position in the church was due mainly to the fact that he was the Lord's brother. During Jesus' life-time he had held aloof, but had afterwards joined himself to the disciples, and became their leader by a sort of hereditary right.

The position of James was firmly established after the persecution which broke out in 42 A. D. Herod Agrippa, grandson of Herod the Great, had been appointed king of Judaea by the Romans, and sought to ingratiate himself with his subjects by an effort to suppress the Christian movement. As king he had the power of life and death which had been denied to the Jewish council, and the new persecution was far more serious than that which followed the death of Stephen. James the brother of John was put to the sword. Peter himself was thrown into prison, and was only saved from death by an escape which was set down to miracle. The persecution was of short duration, but while it lasted had shattered the church. When the storm had swept by and the Christian cause in Jerusalem was re-constituted the more liberal elements had grown weak. James, with his pronounced legalism, was the undisputed head.

Paul and Barnabas, then, came up to Jerusalem and the memorable Council took place. One account of it is given in Acts xv; another, considerably different, in Paul's Epistle to the Galatians (ii. 1–10). They agree, however, in the main point—that after full discussion with the leading Apostles Paul was allowed the liberty he demanded. According to Acts this was qualified by the proviso that the Gentiles should still observe those parts of the Law which had to do with animal food and the marriage relation. Perhaps at a later time there was an effort to enforce some restriction of this kind, but Paul expressly says that at the Council "nothing was added." The agreement was simply that Paul and Barnabas should be left free to present their gospel to the Gentiles, while the Law should still be binding on the Jews. Paul had thus won his point, and the way was now clear for a Gentile mission. But the decision was at best a compromise, since the question of principle had not been determined. The Jewish section of

FIRST AGE OF CHRISTIANITY 131

the church continued to hold the Law, and the Gentiles could not but feel that their own Christianity was incomplete. Although permitted to dispense with the Law they were tacitly placed on a lower level than the original Jewish converts. Moreover the terms of the decision were ambiguous. The mission was divided into two spheres, but were these to be understood in a racial or a geographical sense? Was the Law to be imposed on all Jews, wherever they might be, or only on Jews within the borders of Palestine?

It was through this ambiguity that trouble arose, almost immediately. Peter paid a visit to Antioch, doubtless with the friendly intention of confirming the good relations which had been arranged at the Council. At first he associated freely with the Gentiles, eating along with them as he could not have done if the observance of the Law had still been a matter of conscience with him. But after the arrival of certain friends of James he returned to the Jewish practice of eating apart, and his example prevailed on other members of the church, and even on Barnabas. It was clear to Paul that the unity of the church was in peril. All the churches outside of Palestine consisted both of Jews and Gentiles, and the two sections would be unable henceforth to hold fellowship, even in the Lord's Supper. Paul therefore stood up in the general meeting of the church and denounced Peter to his face, accusing him of hypocrisy and of compelling the Gentiles to forego their freedom.[15] We do not

---
[15] Gal. ii. 11-14.

know the issue of this memorable dispute. It cannot have caused any lasting bitterness between the two great Apostles, for Paul in his Epistles alludes to Peter with respect and friendliness. But it is significant that Peter from this time on ceases to play an important part in the history. He met with the fate which overtakes all leaders who take a step backward when the moment has come to advance. The great enterprise henceforth went on without him.

(5) THE GREAT MISSION

It was probably the dispute at Antioch which caused Paul and Barnabas to part company. They had arranged to set out on another and more extended missionary tour, but on the eve of starting they quarrelled. The point at issue, according to Acts, was as to whether Mark, who had deserted them on the previous journey, should again go with them. Paul refused to allow him a second chance, while his uncle Barnabas was confident, and as the event proved, rightly, that he would now do faithful service in the cause. A personal difference of this kind may have brought matters to a head, but we may be pretty certain that the quarrel lay deeper. The two Apostles had discovered that on vital questions they no longer saw eye to eye, and felt it better to separate. Paul took as his companion Silas, also called Silvanus, a member of the Jerusalem church who had come to Antioch, and who had been attracted to the new type of Christianity when Barnabas, its former champion, had changed to the other side. Like Paul himself Silas was a Roman citizen, and this would make him the more desirable as a fellow-traveller in strange lands, where it might be necessary sometimes to ask for official protection.

From Antioch Paul and Silas proceeded by land through Cilicia, to the cities visited on the former journey. The little Christian communities were found to be still flourishing, and at Lystra Paul met with a young convert, Timothy, who pleased him so much that he took him as his personal assistant. From the outset it had been Paul's intention to make for the West, but his plans were still vague, and he allowed himself to be guided from stage to stage by those visions and impulses which he attributed to the Spirit. In this manner the missionaries were finally led to Troas, a seaport town near the site of ancient Troy; and here Paul had the most momentous of his visions. In a dream he saw a man beckoning him over to Macedonia, and in obedience to this heavenly sign he decided to carry the gospel into Europe.

Both the hopefulness and the difficulty of this venture were apparent from his experiences in Philippi, the first European city in which he worked. His message met with an eager response, and he founded a church which was henceforth more warmly attached to him than any of his churches. But before long the missionaries came into conflict with powerful interests, and were scourged and imprisoned, and were only set free when they disclosed their Roman citizenship. They went on to Thessalonica, already a great commercial city, as it has been ever since. Here they made a considerable stay and founded a church, but the work was again interrupted. The ominous cry which was to cost the church so much suffering in the next three centuries was raised for the first time —that the Christians were disloyal to the state, obeying "another king, one Jesus."[16] Expelled from Thessalonica the Apostles went on to Beroea, and at this point Paul, worn out by the incessant journeying, proceeded by sea to Athens, where he was to wait for his companions. Athens at this time had lost all its political importance and was purely a city of culture, which by its beauty and its glorious past had attracted wealthy idlers from all parts of the world. Paul here encountered his most notable failure. The intellectuals of the city were at first impressed by him and invited him to set forth his views in the Areopagus, the usual place for philosophical debate. But when they found that what he had to offer was not a new and interesting speculation but an earnest religion they were disappointed, and politely dismissed him. He passed on to Corinth in a mood of deep depression. Athens was the representative Greek city, and had proved wholly indifferent to his message. His great European adventure seemed to have failed.

At Corinth, however, he met from the first with remarkable success. He continued to work in the city and neighborhood for eighteen months, and gathered around him the converts whom we know

---

[16] Ac. xvii. 7.

FIRST AGE OF CHRISTIANITY 135

so well from the Corinthian letters, fickle and unruly, prone at times to fall back on Pagan morals and modes of thinking, but full of enthusiasm for the new teaching. At Corinth Paul was singularly happy not only in his work but in his private life. Through his occupation as a tent-maker he had fallen in with a Jewish couple, Aquila and Priscilla, of the same trade, and made his home with them. They became his converts and his most devoted friends and helpers.

It was at Corinth that Paul wrote the first of his extant Epistles, the earliest writing in the New Testament. He was anxious about the community he had left at Thessalonica, and had sent Timothy to discover whether it had survived the danger which had threatened it. Timothy returned with good news, but reported that the little church was perplexed by religious difficulties. The Thessalonians had understood from Paul's teaching that Christ was to appear immediately and transport them living into his Kingdom. But meanwhile several members of their company had died: would these beloved friends have no part in Christ at his coming? Paul deals in the letter with this difficulty, which must have been a very real one among the earliest Christians. He presents his ideas of the future in a clearer light, and takes occasion to impress anew on his readers the truths of the gospel as he had proclaimed them. The Epistle is peculiarly interesting since it is addressed to recent converts, who were still unversed in the higher doctrines. Better than any other Epistle it reflects to us the nature of Paul's ordinary teaching. We are not to think of him as speaking always in a lofty theological strain. When he tried to interpret the gospel to those who listened to it for the first time he used simple thought and language, and dwelt only on the great outstanding facts. The second Epistle to Thessalonians seems to have been written only a few weeks after the first, and deals with another misunderstanding which had grown out of Paul's teaching on the future. Some members of the Thessalonian church, believing that the return of Christ was just at hand, had fallen into habits of idleness. Why should they waste their labor since all earthly things were presently to lose their value? Paul tells them in a curious apocalyptic chapter that the end cannot come until the final battle has been fought out between Christ and "the man of sin," who will incarnate in himself the forces of evil.[17] This conception of an "Antichrist," as we shall see, plays a great part in the book of Revelation, and some scholars have decided that Paul cannot have entertained it, and that II Thessalonians is not an authentic letter. But there is no reason to doubt that Paul shared in the beliefs common to the early church, and the letter, in all respects, is characteristic of him. It illustrates the sobriety of judgment which he always preserved amidst all his fancies and enthusiasms. However near the end of the world might be he saw clearly

---

[17] II Thess. ii. 2.

that honest labor must ever be necessary to the Christian life.

Paul left Corinth to pay a visit to Jerusalem, for what purpose we do not know. Very likely he had become aware that the extreme Jewish party was seeking to thwart his work, and thought he might check the mischief at the fountain-head. On his voyage he made a brief stay at Ephesus, and decided that this great city, one of the chief meeting-places of East and West, would be his next field of labor. Meanwhile he called on Aquila and Priscilla to prepare the ground for him, and completed his journey to Jerusalem. He returned by land, in order to re-visit his old friends at Antioch and the churches he had founded in Southern Asia Minor. Arriving in Ephesus he found that Aquila and Priscilla had worked to good purpose, and had made at least one very notable convert, a learned and eloquent Alexandrian Jew named Apollos. They were so much impressed by his gifts that they had sent him to Corinth to carry on the work of Paul, and at Corinth he won conspicuous success. A party formed around him which acclaimed him as far superior to Paul. It is worth observing that Paul never expresses any jealousy of those rivals who supplanted him from time to time. With his imperious spirit he was not an easy man to work with, and sometimes speaks harshly of old friends. But his quarrels were never the result of personal jealousy. From this and the kindred vices of small natures he was entirely free.

His first converts at Ephesus were a group of men whom the author of Acts appears to think of as Christians, although they had not yet heard of the coming of the Holy Spirit and knew only the baptism of John.[18] There is good reason to believe that they were really adherents of John the Baptist, whose sect had maintained itself after his death, and had somehow found a home in Ephesus. In this connection it is interesting to note that the Fourth Gospel, written at Ephesus half a century afterwards, is concerned to prove that John, although a great prophet, was inferior to Jesus and must be regarded merely as his forerunner.[19] This peculiarity of the Gospel may be explained in the light of that episode in Acts, from which we may infer that John's followers were numerous in Ephesus, and that an effort was made to win them for the church.

Paul's stay at Ephesus extended to three years. During this time he worked not only in the city itself but in the whole Roman province of Asia, of which it was the capital. The measure of his success is given us by the fact that in the next generation this province had become the centre of Christianity, and in several directions exerted a decisive influence on its whole future. Very little is told us in Acts of this all-important period of Paul's career, but from references in his own Epistles we know that in Ephesus he was exposed to grave danger, and was only saved by the brave inter-

---
[18] Ac. xix. 1–5.
[19] Cf. Jn. i. 8, 15; iii, 27 ff.; v. 32–36.

FIRST AGE OF CHRISTIANITY 139

vention of Aquila and Priscilla.[20] He "fought with wild beasts at Ephesus,"[21] perhaps literally in the amphitheatre, more likely in the figurative sense that he was maltreated by a savage mob. It is significant that from this time on he appears to give up his hope that he will survive till the Lord's coming. He had now looked death in the face, and could not but feel ever afterwards that his life hung by a thread.

Not only was he threatened by personal danger but during this Ephesian period he was in constant anxiety about his churches. Ever since the Council of Jerusalem he had been regarded with suspicion by the Jewish Christians, and an organized movement had now begun to counteract his work. Emissaries from Jerusalem visited the communities he had founded and tried to discredit him as a mere adventurer, who had no authority to preach a gospel divorced from the Law. Paul naturally speaks with much bitterness of these opponents, and their efforts to raise doubts in the ill-instructed minds of the Gentiles were certainly unpardonable. But they doubtless believed quite sincerely that the Gentiles were being deluded into an imperfect Christianity and were in need of fuller light. It does not appear that the leading Apostles were in sympathy with their attitude, much less with their onslaught on Paul; yet those obviously earnest men could not be refused "letters of commendation"[22]

[20] Rom. xvi. 3, 4.
[21] I Cor. xv. 32.
[22] II Cor. iii. 1.

which certified that they were highly esteemed in the Jerusalem church. This it was that made their propaganda so dangerous. Wherever they went they were able to represent themselves as spokesmen for the mother-church, duly accredited by the foremost Apostles.

The trouble first broke out in Galatia. This name belonged in the strict sense to a region in the north of Asia Minor, which there is no evidence that Paul had ever visited. Most scholars are now agreed that the name is applied to the Roman province of Galatia, including the southern district as well as the northern. In other words the Galatian churches were those which Paul and Barnabas had founded in the course of their first journey. The Jewish emissaries had found their way into these churches and had won them over. It was reported to Paul at Ephesus that his Galatian converts had turned against him, and would have nothing to do with a gospel which disowned the Law. He forthwith wrote his Epistle to the Galatians, in some respects the most vital and characteristic of all his letters. He dictated it, as his custom was, but before closing seized the pen himself and added "in large letters," (the ancient equivalent for italics), a few fiery sentences in which he gave vent to his personal feelings.[23] The letter all through is written under strong emotion. Not only was Paul wounded in his affections by the revolt of his converts, but he saw plainly that his whole work and the whole future of Christianity were at stake.

---
[23] Gal. vi. 11.

If the gospel was to be a mere appanage of the Law there was no gospel. The Epistle is the most striking statement of the Pauline theology, and as such was adopted by Luther as the Magna Charta of the Reformation. It has also a supreme value from an historical point of view. In replying to the insinuations of his enemies Paul takes occasion in the first two chapters to review his own life and the early days of the church. These chapters may be regarded as the bed-rock of New Testament history—an incontrovertible record of the main events by the man who knew them best.

During his stay at Ephesus Paul also suffered a growing anxiety on behalf of the Corinthian church. From his own references we know that he wrote at least two letters to Corinth in addition to the two which we now possess.[24] The correspondence began with one of those lost letters, a fragment of which is perhaps preserved in II Cor. vi. 11–vii. 1. The Corinthians answered it, seeking the advice of Paul on several urgent problems, and just about the same time he had visitors from Corinth who brought disquieting reports.[25] Such was the origin of our First Epistle to the Corinthians. Paul takes up, one after another, the various matters to which his attention had been called, and the Epistle thus falls into a number of sections, with no central theme. But just for this reason it is the richest and most interesting of the Epistles, enabling us, as in a series of moving pictures, to realize the life

---

[24] Cf. I Cor. v. 9; II Cor. ii. 3, 4.
[25] I Cor. i. 11.

of an early Christian community in all its aspects. Some of the questions with which Paul deals (*e.g.* Is it right to eat food which had been offered to idols? Ought a Christian woman to marry a heathen? How ought the "spiritual gifts" to be estimated?) have long ceased to perplex us; but even on these problems of his own day Paul never fails to throw out ideas of far-reaching import. It was characteristic of the man that he was never satisfied until he had run back even a minor issue to some great guiding principle. In another respect, too, these more ephemeral sections of the Epistle have a permanent value. The great task which confronted the early missionaries was that of applying the gospel precepts to conditions which Jesus himself had never contemplated. With wonderful insight Paul seizes on the inner principles of the teaching, and shows how they are valid, not merely for peasant life in Galilee, but for the complex civilization of a great Gentile city. We can still learn from this Epistle how the Sermon on the Mount may be applied and re-interpreted in view of the many-sided demands of our own day. In I Corinthians, however, Paul discusses not only the special difficulties of a given church but some of the highest themes of religion. The fifteenth chapter contains his fullest teaching on immortality. The praise of Christian love in the thirteenth chapter comes nearer to the very heart of the gospel than anything outside of the words of Jesus. It may be noted, too, that in I Corinthians there are two passages of cardinal historical value—the account

FIRST AGE OF CHRISTIANITY 143

of the institution of the Lord's Supper (xi.23-26) and the record of Jesus' appearances after his death (xv.3-8). When we remember that Paul wrote the Epistle less than twenty-five years after the Crucifixion—a generation earlier than our earliest Gospel—the importance of his testimony is at once manifest.

In I Corinthians Paul had found it necessary to warn his readers against certain dangers into which they were drifting. With their Greek individualism they were breaking up into cliques and parties;[26] with the pride of intellect which was also Greek they were turning Christianity into a mere speculation, to the neglect of those moral qualities on which Jesus had laid the chief stress.[27] These evils during the year or more which followed became more pronounced, and the situation was aggravated by the arrival of those Jewish emissaries who had wrought such havoc in Galatia. In the midst of his troubles at Ephesus Paul learned that his Corinthian church had shaken off his authority. He sent one of his trusted assistants, or perhaps made a flying visit himself, to bring it to a better mind, but was only answered by insult. In a bitter and indignant mood he wrote another letter to assert his claim on the disloyal church and shame it into repentance. It is not improbable that chapters ten to thirteen of the Epistle known as II Corinthians are part of this letter, which was long supposed to be lost. As the Epistle now stands these last four

---
[26] I Cor. iii. 4 ff.
[27] I Cor. xii. 31; xiv. 12.

chapters are in complete contrast to those which precede them, and their tone and purport are exactly those of the "painful letter" as Paul himself describes it. No sooner had the letter been despatched than Paul would fain have recalled it, fearing that it would only defeat its own end and harden the Corinthians in their rebellious mood. His closing weeks at Ephesus were darkened with this anxiety over the church which had been the proudest trophy of his missionary life.

We learn from Acts that the work at Ephesus came to an abrupt end. The city was famous all over the world for the great temple of Artemis, and much of its wealth was derived from the sale of souvenirs to pilgrims and tourists. For some reason the trade had latterly fallen off, and the craftsmen, looking about for a scapegoat, chose to lay the blame on the new Christian movement. They raised an uproar which might easily have led to a serious riot if the magistrates had not promptly interfered. Paul recognized that it was wise for him to leave the city immediately. An inquiry into the cause of the late excitement would be held, and his name certainly brought forward. The old danger from which he had so narrowly escaped would press upon him again in a more serious form.

His purpose when he left Ephesus was to make for Corinth and see if he could effect anything by his personal influence. But he felt that the visit was useless until he knew what reception had been given to his letter, and he therefore waited in Philippi while Titus went on before him to explore the ground. Titus at last returned with the good news that the Corinthians were ashamed of their treatment of the Apostle, and were now eager to welcome him. With an overflowing heart he wrote the Epistle known as II Corinthians.[28] His object is to make it clear that he bears no grudge, and wishes to have the differences of the last few months completely forgotten when he comes. II Corinthians is the most intensely personal of Paul's Epistles. More than any other it reveals the great heart of the man, his glowing affection for his spiritual children, his utter self-forgetfulness in his work for the gospel.

Paul lingered for a while in Macedonia before proceeding to Corinth. His object was partly to allow the letter of reconciliation to produce its full effect, and partly to complete an enterprise which had occupied him for some years past, and of which he has much to say in II Corinthians. At the Council of Jerusalem he had promised that the Gentile churches should contribute to the support of the poor in the mother-church,[29] and this enterprise had assumed increasing importance in his eyes. For one thing he felt the need of assuring the Jewish Christians, by a tangible proof, that the Gentiles of whom they were so suspicious were in full sympathy with them. At the same time he welcomed the opportunity of uniting his various churches in a work of beneficence. Ideally the church formed

---
[28] II Cor. ii. 12 ff.
[29] Gal. ii. 10.

a single brotherhood, but as yet it consisted of a number of scattered communities without any visible bond. Paul with his statesmanlike vision was planning to draw them more closely together. His scheme for the collection was the first step towards that federation which was to make the church the mightiest power in the world.

It was arranged that delegates from each of the leading churches should join Paul at Corinth and travel with him to Jerusalem. The presence of all these representatives would give significance to the gift, and would also serve to place the conduct of Paul himself above suspicion. His enemies, as he well knew, were ready to avail themselves of any handle against him, and if he was left in sole charge of a considerable sum of money they would find occasion for all sorts of calumny. He duly arrived at Corinth, and had three months to wait before the delegates joined him. For the first time in many years he enjoyed a brief period of rest, all the more welcome as he had lately undergone such a terrible strain. It was in this tranquil interval that he wrote the Epistle to the Romans, the longest and most elaborate of his letters. If we had known nothing of its origin we should have gathered, from the character of the Epistle itself, that it was written with a serene mind. Paul finds himself at leisure to think out his ideas and to present them according to a reasoned plan.

He composes the letter with more than his usual care since he is writing to a church as yet unknown to him—a church, too, which he respects above all

FIRST AGE OF CHRISTIANITY 147

others because of its connection with the imperial city. It had been his lifelong dream to visit Rome, and now he had designed, after his journey to Jerusalem, to close his labors in the east and begin an extensive mission in the west.[30] For this purpose he wished to make sure beforehand of the full support of the Roman church, which would necessarily be the base of his operations. He knew that at Rome as elsewhere his work had been misrepresented, and this is doubtless one reason why his letter takes the form of a full exposition of his Christian teaching. In view, too, of his projected mission he feels it necessary to set forth his conception of the gospel as a message for all mankind. He says in effect to the Roman Christians "You are bound to help me in the work I am undertaking. The religion you profess is universal by its very nature, and you have no right to keep it to yourselves." The Epistle, therefore, is not a mere theological treatise, but is meant to serve a highly practical purpose. As an active missionary Paul sets himself to prove that the gospel, and the gospel alone can offer salvation to the world. All other methods have failed. The Gentiles, seeking God by the natural light of reason, have fallen into ever-deepening corruption. The Jews, relying on the Law, have found that it only mocked them by holding up an ideal to which they cannot attain. The one true way to salvation has at last been opened up to men in the gospel. Through Christ God has revealed Himself as the God of mercy, who will

---
[30] Rom. xv. 23 ff.

accept us on the one condition of faith. Not only so, but through Christ we receive the Spirit, which makes possible for us that new life of holiness which we can never achieve for ourselves.

It is evident that although he had not yet visited Rome, Paul was well-informed on the conditions in the Roman church. Much of the obscurity of the Epistle is due to our ignorance of the local situation which he keeps in view as he writes. From chapters fourteen and fifteen we can gather that the church was divided into two parties—a Gentile majority, contemptuous of Jewish prejudices, whom he calls "the strong," and a Jewish minority, "the weak," who were still troubled with scruples about forbidden meats and holy days.[81] In asserting the claims of faith as against the Law Paul is careful to repress the Gentile arrogance. Faith is the one condition of salvation and the Gentiles have responded to this condition, but they are none the less to acknowledge the unique place which God has accorded to Israel. This double motive runs through all the Epistle. In Galatians Paul appears as the uncompromising foe of Judaism. In Romans he takes pains to do justice to it, while still insisting on the primacy of faith.

(6) THE CAPTIVITY AND DEATH OF PAUL

Paul's companions at last joined him and he set out for Jerusalem. His intention was to sail direct from Corinth, but he learned of a plot to intercept him, perhaps for the sake of the money which was

---
[81] Rom. xiv. 1-6; xv. 1.

FIRST AGE OF CHRISTIANITY 149

in his keeping. At the last moment he changed his route and travelled to Macedonia, then along the coast of Asia Minor, and so to Tyre and Caesarea. In this manner he was able on the way to visit a number of the churches he had founded and which he was not likely to see again. His plans were arranged for the new mission to the West, but he had a presentiment that something would happen to him at Jerusalem which might prevent him from entering on it. These fears were shared by the friends whom he encountered on the way.[32] Every one knew that feeling at Jerusalem ran strongly against him. Again and again he had come into violent collision with the Jewish synagogue, and was notorious as a renegade to the Law, a subverter of all that his countrymen most revered. Now he was going to Jerusalem, the headquarters of Jewish bigotry. It hardly required the foresight of the Christian prophets to know that he would incur danger.

After a few days' rest at Caesarea the party went on to Jerusalem. Nothing is told us of the presentation of the gift, but we know that Paul was well received by the leading Apostles. They recommended, however, that in order to satisfy the Jewish party he should stand sponsor to four men who had a vow to discharge in the temple. This was a work of charity often undertaken by pious Jews, and by performing it Paul would convince his opponents that he had not broken with the sacred customs. He readily consented, but his well-meant effort to

[32] Ac. xx. 38; xxi. 10 ff.

be conciliatory brought him to disaster. Jews from Asia Minor saw him entering the temple with his clients, and raised the cry that this friend of the Gentiles was now introducing them into the holy place. A tumult arose in which the mob would have torn him in pieces if he had not been rescued by the Roman garrison and placed under arrest. From that moment he was never to be a free man again.

His supposed offence had been committed in the temple, and he was therefore brought to trial before the Jewish council. The case was remanded, and meanwhile a nephew of Paul informed him that a plot was on foot to assassinate him before the next hearing. As a result of this warning he was sent under a strong guard to Caesarea, the seat of the Roman governor, where the trial could be conducted dispassionately. Felix, the governor, was the brother of the court favourite, Pallas, of evil repute in Roman history. He owed his appointment to his brother's influence, and was notoriously worthless and incompetent—"a man," says Tacitus in one of his immortal epigrams, "who exercised a kingly office in the spirit of a slave." Felix was quick to perceive that Paul was an important man among the Christians, who might be willing to pay a considerable bribe for his acquittal. Instead of pronouncing judgment at once he therefore allowed the case to stand over for two years, and all this time Paul remained a prisoner at Caesarea. At last, with the accession of the emperor Nero, the old officials were dismissed, and Felix was replaced by

Festus, a man of very different stamp. As soon as he came into office he ordered the long-deferred trial to be held, and it would almost certainly have ended in Paul's deliverance. But during the long imprisonment he had grown weary. He had despaired of ever getting justice in the corrupt courts of Judaea, and had resolved to exercise his privilege as a Roman citizen and appeal to the supreme court at Rome. So when brought before Festus he uttered the potent formula "Caesarem appello," and as soon as it left his lips no inferior court had any jurisdiction over him. Festus had no choice but to send him direct to Rome.

The story of the voyage is graphically told by the author of Acts, who was himself one of Paul's party. He describes how the ship, overtaken by a premature winter storm, was driven out of its course, and for fourteen days was at the mercy of the wind in an unknown sea. It was one of those desperate emergencies when all artificial distinctions are forgotten, and men take rank according to the sheer qualities of their manhood. Paul had come on board as one of a batch of prisoners; before the voyage ended he was the virtual ruler of the ship, and thanks to him it finally reached a bay in Malta, without the loss of a single life. The rest of the winter was spent in the island, and he was then transported to Italy, and was conducted along the Appian Way from Puteoli to Rome.

For three years more he remained a prisoner. There was always a congestion of business in the supreme court, and Paul had to wait his turn.

Although a prisoner he was allowed a considerable degree of freedom. He lived in a room of his own near the barracks, with a soldier attached to him night and day by a light chain. A number of old friends had come for his sake to Rome, and through them he was able to take some part in furthering the Christian cause in the city. Even in the military camp to which he was restricted he found opportunities of imparting his message.[33] It is somewhat remarkable that so few of his letters date from the period when he had such ample leisure for literary work. The reason probably is that he had transferred the oversight of his churches to other men, and did not wish to hamper them by his interference. Three or four of the Epistles, however, may be assigned to these closing years, though it has recently been argued, on doubtful grounds, that they were written during his imprisonment in Ephesus or Caesarea.

The two letters to Colossae and to Philemon were sent off together, to the same destination. Colossae was a town about one hundred miles east of Ephesus, which Paul had never visited personally, but which had received the gospel from his disciple Epaphras. Members of the Colossian church had become well known to him, and he was warmly interested in it. Two arrivals at Rome had now drawn his attention to Colossae. Onesimus, a slave of Philemon, had robbed his master and escaped to Rome, where he had fallen in with

---
[33] Phil. i. 12, 13.

FIRST AGE OF CHRISTIANITY 153

Paul and had finally become his devoted friend and servant. About the same time the missionary Epaphras had reached the city, with disquieting news of a strange heresy which had broken out in the Colossian church. Paul was thus led to write two letters. One of them is addressed to Philemon, and begs him to take back Onesimus and treat him as a Christian brother, for such he had now become. It is the shortest of Paul's letters, but illustrates, perhaps better than any other, his tact and kindness, and the personal charm which he exercised. His attitude to slavery in this letter has been the subject of much criticism. We must remember, however, that a crusade against slavery in that age, when the whole structure of society was so closely involved with it, would have done far more harm than good. It may fairly be claimed that although he did not denounce the evil system, Paul prepared the way for its destruction. He demanded in this letter and elsewhere that the slave should be treated as a man, that master and slave alike should regard themselves as servants of Christ. The Epistle to Colossians is of special interest as the first record we have of those false teachings which were to endanger the very existence of the church during the next century. The heresy at Colossae was a peculiar one, in which Jewish and heathen elements were mingled;[84] but there can be little doubt that was an early stage of the Gnostic phase of thought of which we are soon to hear so much. Paul answers it by insisting on the all-sufficient worth of

[84] Cf. Col. ii. 16-21.

Christ. The heretics had taught that he was only one of many angelic powers, to which man must look for salvation. Paul declares that all spiritual forces are gathered up in him. "In him dwells all the fulness of the Godhead bodily."[85]

If the Epistle to Ephesians is by Paul it must have been written at the same time as Colossians, for it presents the same ideas, often in identical words. This similarity has caused many scholars to doubt its genuineness. They hold that it is the work not of Paul but of some disciple of his who had the Colossian letter before him and used it as his groundwork. A still more serious difficulty is the style of the Epistle, with its long, intricate sentences in which the terseness and impetuosity of Paul are entirely wanting. The ideas, however, are Pauline, and the Epistle has a grandeur and elevation which Paul rarely excelled even in his highest moods. Its theme is the sublime calling of the church. In this community of Christ, in which hostile races have been drawn into one brotherhood, the author sees the beginning of a vast work of reconciliation, which will finally embrace the whole universe. God has purposed to bring all things at last into harmony through Christ, and the church, in which warring forces have learned to work together, is the earnest of this great fulfilment. The Epistle may or may not be by Paul; on this point scholars are almost equally divided. But the title "To the Ephesians" is certainly mistaken. The best manuscripts omit the words "in Ephesus" in

[85] Col. i. 16-19; ii. 9.

FIRST AGE OF CHRISTIANITY 155

the first verse, and there is no other evidence for the traditional title. The Epistle contains no greetings or personal messages, and we cannot believe that Paul would write in this detached manner to people with whom he had been closely associated for three years. One theory is that it is the lost letter to the Laodiceans, to which Paul refers in Col. iv. 16. According to another view he wrote it as a circular letter to a number of churches, leaving a blank in the opening verse for the name of each separate church.

It was only fitting that Paul's last letter, written on the very eve of his death, should be to Philippi, the church which he loved above all the others. The Philippians, fearing that he might be destitute in his prison at Rome, had sent him a sum of money, and he writes to thank them for this gift, which had deeply touched him. He assures them, however, that their fears are groundless. He is well cared for and in the midst of friends. He has hopes that in his trial, which is now imminent, he will be acquitted, and that he will shortly return to them. Yet it is clear that although he writes cheerfully, so as not to distress his beloved Philippians, he is prepared for the worst. It is clear, too, that he does not greatly care what the outcome may be.[36] The tone of the letter is that of a weary man, who knows that his work is done and looks forward to his release.

Nothing is definitely known of the time and circumstances of Paul's death. The book of Acts

[36] Phil. i. 20–23.

suddenly breaks off before it reaches the trial, and for later information we are dependent on vague references in the early Fathers. That Paul died a martyr is certain, but it is sometimes maintained that he was acquitted at his first trial and that he commenced the mission in Spain which he had projected. Shortly afterwards, it is supposed, he was re-arrested and sent back to Rome for execution. A theory of this kind is almost necessary if we accept the Epistles to Timothy and Titus (commonly known as the Pastoral Epistles) as the genuine work of Paul; for no place can be found for them in any previous part of his life. It is now generally agreed, however, that these Epistles contain only a few fragments from Paul's hand, and apart from them there is little evidence that he survived his first imprisonment. The very fact that the author of Acts breaks off before the trial is highly significant. One of his chief aims is to show that the Roman government had always been friendly to the Christian missionaries, and if Paul had been acquitted by the highest tribunal of the empire he would certainly have told us.

We may conclude, on every ground, that the trial ended disastrously. The profession of Christianity had not yet become illegal, and the charge on which Paul was condemned would not be that of his religion. He would be judged, rather, as an agitator who had caused riot in various cities of Greece and Asia Minor, and who had finally been arrested in the very act of raising a tumult at Jerusalem. The political situation in Palestine had

FIRST AGE OF CHRISTIANITY 157

become very grave in those years immediately preceding the great revolt, and Roman judges would take a serious view of a disturbance in the center of Jewish disaffection. Paul was condemned, and according to a very ancient tradition was beheaded on the Ostian road, a little way out of the city. The magnificent cathedral of St. Paul's without the Gates marks the spot where he is said to have been buried by his sorrowing companions.

It was not unusual forty or fifty years ago to speak of Paul as the second founder of Christianity. The suggestion was that this great man had taken up the crude belief of an obscure sect, and had transformed it by his genius into a world-wide religion. Paul himself never made this extravagant estimate of his work, and fuller critical inquiry has proved it to be quite mistaken. The Christian ideas and institutions had been matured before Paul came on the scene. The Gentile mission had already taken firm root. Yet his service to Christianity can hardly be overestimated. Though he did not originate the Gentile mission he grounded it in Christian principle, and did more than any other man to advance it. Though he did not create the new beliefs he defined and interpreted them with matchless insight. It has often been held that Paul distorted the gospel by recasting it in Hellenistic moulds, and that our task is to get behind his teaching to that of Jesus. But the truth is that he was the great conservative force in early Christianity. The Hellenizing process was inevitable, and except for Paul it would have been carried out in such a manner as to destroy everything that was distinctively Christian; this, indeed, was what actually happened in the Gnostic schools. Paul was in profound sympathy with the mind of Jesus. Through him the work of interpretation was so effected that the essential truths, instead of falling out of sight, were affirmed more unmistakably. But besides all that Paul definitely accomplished, as missionary and teacher, we must take account of his personality, which was the greatest of all his gifts to the Christian cause. The author of Acts, his friend and biographer, seems to know little about Paul's theology. It is doubtful whether he had ever read any of the Epistles. Yet for Paul the man he has a boundless admiration, and sees in him the living pattern of all that the gospel meant. It was all-important that Christianity at the very outset had its representative in this great man, who by his self-sacrifice, his passion for all that was highest, his sympathy with the poor and weak, his incomparable qualities of mind and heart, made real to the world the message of Jesus. Most of his converts were ignorant men and women who must often have been puzzled by his doctrines. But they could always understand the man. They could respond to his counsel, "Be ye followers of me, even as I am of Christ."

(7) THE CHURCH AFTER PAUL

Paul died, according to the most probable dating, in 62 A. D., and his death marks the close of the early, formative period. The church consisted, as yet, of a number of small communities scattered over a wide area, and comprising perhaps ten thousand people in all. Its members were mostly drawn from the poorer classes, though in each community there were a few men of education and fair social position. Its meetings were held in the rooms of private houses, and it had no regular forms of worship, no literature, no common government. But the foundations had been securely laid, and the next fifty years witnessed an amazing progress. At the close of this second period Christianity had spread itself everywhere. The little handfuls of believers had grown into large communities, drawn from all classes and combining in an ever closer organization. The time was in sight when the church was to stand forth as the rival of the empire. Unfortunately this period of expansion is very imperfectly known to us. The work was now carried on not by a few men of heroic stature who left a vivid memory to after times, but by thousands of ordinary men and women. They lived, on the whole, under peaceful conditions, and seemed at the time to be doing nothing that was worthy of record. Scarcely a name or an incident out of that marvelously fruitful period was remembered in the next generation. It is not possible, therefore, to trace the progress of the church in this age as in that which had preceded it. We must be content to mark the general movement, as it is reflected in the New Testament literature, and even this can only be done in bare outline.

Two events, both destined to have a profound effect on the future of the church, took place shortly after the death of Paul. (1) In the year 64 A. D. Rome was destroyed by fire, and a rumour arose that the emperor Nero himself, in one of his mad escapades, was responsible for the disaster. To divert the popular suspicion he accused the Christians, whose strange ideas and customs had marked them out as a peculiar and most likely a dangerous sect. They were arrested in large numbers, and after trial on the flimsiest evidence were put to death with fiendish cruelty on the Vatican hill, from which the Roman bishops were afterwards to rule the world. According to a tradition which runs back to such an early time that it may be authentic, Peter himself was one of the victims of this massacre. The outbreak only lasted a few days and was confined to Rome, but it had far-reaching consequences. It gave a preëminence, never afterwards lost, to the Roman church, which had nobly suffered in the cause of Christ. It lifted the new religion out of obscurity, and so helped on its progress. Above all, it created a gulf between Christianity and the State. The church now looked on the empire as its enemy, while the empire was ready at any moment to persecute the church. (2) The other momentous event was the destruction of Jerusalem by Titus in 70 A. D. By this calamity the church was not directly affected, for the Christians were opposed to the revolt and had migrated from the city in a body before the siege began. Yet the fall of Jerusalem changed the

FIRST AGE OF CHRISTIANITY 161

whole outlook for Christianity. Hitherto, although its progress was chiefly among the Gentiles it was linked with its Jewish past. The Christian communities everywhere looked to Jerusalem as their centre and deferred to its leading. With the fall of the city the prestige of the mother-church was gone. Jewish Christianity, which in Paul's lifetime had been such a potent force, ceased to have any importance.

We know almost nothing, then, of the history of the church during the fifty years after Paul's death. But when the curtain is again lifted we see that the period has witnessed mighty changes. In the light of them we can infer, at least in a general way, what has been happening in the obscure interval.

(1) The converts were always increasing in number, but still belonged, for the most part, to the great cities. Paul, in his anxiety to spread the knowledge of the gospel as rapidly as possible had confined his work to the cities, and this policy was continued in the years that followed. For a long time to come Christianity, which had begun among the villages of Galilee, was in the main a city religion. It still made its strongest appeal to the poorer classes, but as it became better known it drew adherents from a wider circle. Men of philosophical and literary culture were attracted by it. It made converts, not always to its advantage, among the wealthy and powerful. Towards the end of the century several members of the imperial

house seem to have secretly embraced the new religion.

(2) The great majority of Christians were now Gentile, and this influx of converts who had so recently been heathen constituted a serious danger. Most of them, it cannot be doubted, were of an earnest religious spirit. They were alive to the beauty and grandeur of the new teaching, and often proved their sincerity by suffering on its behalf. But inevitably they carried over with them many of the ideas and beliefs which they had held as Pagans. Christian doctrine, as we shall see later, was profoundly modified by this infusion of Gentile thought. Christian worship, too, began to turn more and more on the Sacraments, which were now invested with a mystical significance, like the corresponding rites in the heathen religions. At the same time we have to recognize that without this modification the gospel could not have conquered the Roman world. So long as it was conveyed in Jewish forms of thought it was exotic. Now it had become assimilated to the Gentile culture, and found a natural entrance into the Gentile mind.

(3) The church was gradually building up a system of government. At first it had been a free brotherhood, impatient of all that savoured of regulation. Its acknowledged leaders were not officials, but men who were obviously gifted with the Spirit in a singular degree. They were not attached to any locality, but wandered from place to place at their own will. These travelling mis-

FIRST AGE OF CHRISTIANITY 163

sionaries were of several grades—Apostles, Prophets or Teachers—according to the gifts which they possessed;[87] and assumed the oversight for the time being of any church which they happened to visit. Even in Paul's day this loose organization was proving insufficient. The churches needed leaders, endowed with the necessary authority, who were always on the spot, and Paul usually took measures to appoint such leaders. As far as possible he gave them directions, by letter or by a visit from one of his assistants, but for the most part they had the management of affairs in their own hands. These local officials, as was only natural, became jealous of interference from the outside.[88] Paul himself had frequent difficulties with them, and after his death, when the communities had grown large and important, and the itinerant teachers were no longer men of commanding influence, the old system proved unworkable. The government of the churches came to be left entirely to the local overseers or "bishops." At first they acted as a board, but there was invariably some one man of strong personality who took the lead, and his authority in course of time assumed an official character. The other "elders" became merely the assessors of the one ruling "bishop." This system of one-man government, which was to culminate a few centuries later in the Roman papacy, was gradually establishing itself in the later New Testament period. In its early days the church had placed all

---
[87] I Cor. xii. 28; Eph. iv. 11.
[88] Cf. III John v. 9.

its members on a footing of perfect equality. It had opposed itself to all forms of organization, so that everything might be ordered by the direct guidance of the Spirit. Now, under pressure of circumstances, it was subjecting itself to a fixed order of government. The free brotherhood of disciples was to develope erelong into the most highly organized society that the world has known.

(4) As it perfected its mode of government the church extended and systematized its practical activities. From the outset it had been much more than an association for worship. We have seen that in the first days at Jerusalem the disciples had called themselves "brethren," and had made the community responsible for the welfare of its poorer members. This side of Christian duty continued to be emphasized. The virtue most highly esteemed was that of "brotherly love"—sympathy with all fellow-Christians, and especially those in need. Since the church was mainly recruited from the poor, and its members had often to suffer for their faith, there was ample scope for this practical religion. Every church was expected to collect money for the relief of those who were in need. Special officers were set apart to administer this fund, and the women of the church, especially unmarried women and widows, who were free from household cares, took a leading part in the works of charity. We are wont to think of the "institutional church" as a peculiar product of our own times, but in the first century the church was institutional, to a far greater extent than it has ever

been since. The lot of the poor man in Roman times was a hard, and often a desperate one. When he entered the church he found himself welcomed into a great friendly society. It looked after him when he was sick, found him employment, freed him from the debtor's prison, provided for his family after his death. The age was one of constant travel, and the Christian, wherever he went, had only to introduce himself to the local church to be sure of hospitality. So many were the advantages which the church offered to its members that it had constantly to be on its guard against impostors; and in spite of all precautions it had numerous converts on its roll who had little interest in its religious message. But it had no cause to regret its liberality. By its works of practical kindness, more even than by its teaching, it made the purpose of Jesus real to men, and leavened the Pagan world with his spirit.

(5) The chief danger which beset the church during those years of progress was from the inroads of heresy. We have seen that one of Paul's last letters was directed against "false teachers" who had appeared at Colossae. They proved to be the harbingers of a great movement which threatened the church for more than a century, and seemed likely at on time to submerge it altogether. Little is known in detail of the origin and progress of this Gnostic movement, but we can at least surmise how it arose. As a result of the mingling of East and West—Oriental mysticism and Greek philosophy—the air had been full for a long time past of re-

ligious speculation. There were men everywhere—sometimes charlatans like Simon Magus in Samaria, sometimes highly gifted thinkers—who were advancing theories of the origin of evil and the destiny of the soul and the nature of divine being. Their usual method was to borrow suggestions from the various mythologies of the time, and to work them into new combinations with the aid of Greek metaphysical ideas. Those speculative minds were not slow to perceive the possibilities of the Christian message. As preached by the Apostles it appeared too crude and simple, but manifestly it offered some great conceptions which could be made the basis of an imposing system. On all sides there arose new versions of Christianity, in which fragments of the gospel were ingeniously blended with Pagan imaginations. Christ was transformed into a half-abstract divine principle, who had appeared for a brief season in the semblance of a human life. He was associated with mysterious events in the invisible world, and was supposed to have divulged a secret revelation to chosen disciples in the interval between his death and ascension. A large literature grew up which professed to hand down this revelation, and in private meetings strange rites were practised, and pass-words and magic formulae were communicated to those who were deemed worthy. This mode of belief which grew up in the later part of the first century was more Pagan than Christian. Some of the many Gnostic systems frankly discarded the moral law, on the ground that it was imposed by the God of the Old Testament, from whose tyranny Christ had set men free. Others demanded an asceticism of the extremest type. Yet the Gnostic teaching, with its air of mystery and its pretensions to a deep wisdom had a marvelous fascination for numbers of Christian people. The later writers of the New Testament all find it necessary to combat the heresy, which threatened to break up the church and to destroy the whole meaning of the gospel.

This conflict with the false teachings had several momentous results. (1) A powerful impetus was given to the formation of an official ministry, under a single head. It was found that when authority was divided among a number of men, all representing different opinions, there was no guarantee against the entrance of heresy. If a church was to hold together in face of the disruptive forces which were now at work it needed to have one leader, well-grounded in the faith and clothed with ample powers. (2) The beliefs of the church were now defined in a settled form. In the early days the conception of orthodoxy, as it was afterwards understood, had not arisen. The convert was required at baptism to make the confession "Jesus is Lord," and to accept the outstanding beliefs which distinguished Christians from Jews and heathen. But beyond this point he was left free. Within the church there were many types of thought, widely differing from each other and all legitimate. This liberty was not only permitted but encouraged. Each Christian was supposed to have the gift of the Spirit, by which he could interpret the message for himself, according to his own measure of grace. To this freedom we owe the freshness and richness and sincerity of early Christian thought, as we find it in the New Testament. The false teachers, however, had abused their freedom; and if the distinctive Christian beliefs were not to evaporate altogether they had to be carefully defined. The time was still distant when formal creeds were drawn up, clause by clause, to which every Christian was bound to subscribe, on peril of excommunication. But already we begin to hear of the "confession," the "rule of faith." Orthodoxy, as opposed to the vagaries of the Gnostic teachers, has become one of the essential marks of the Christian. (3) Perhaps the most important of all the results of the combat with heresy was the formation of the New Testament. If error was to be held in check there needed to be fixed standards to which the church could appeal, and these were found in the Gospel history and in the writings of the Apostles. The need was all the more imperative as the heretics had writings of their own, to which the names of revered leaders were often falsely attached. If these forgeries were not to work mischief the genuine writings had to be sifted out and set apart. Hitherto the church had used the Old Testament as its sacred book, expounding the prophecies in the light of their Christian fulfilment. Now it collected its own early records, and gave them the rank of Scripture. The New Testament came into being.

Such were the various moments which marked the period after Paul's death. They were all aspects of one great movement—the building of what is known as the Catholic Church. In the previous age each community had stood by itself. There was a cleavage between the Jewish and the Gentile sections of the church, and in every community there were parties, like those of Paul and Apollos and Cephas at Corinth. An intelligent observer, at the time of Paul's death, would doubtless have foretold that the new religion, in spite of its wonderful progress, would soon disintegrate into a number of petty sects. But after Paul a movement set in towards uniformity. A new generation had arrived, to which the question of the Law and similar issues meant little. Difficulties had now beset the church in the face of which it could not afford to be disunited. Formerly the communities had been jealous for their independence, but the new ideal that hovered before the minds of all Christians was that of a universal church, with one type of government, one form of worship, one confession of faith.

This progress towards unity was hastened by the common danger in which the whole church was involved as the State became increasingly hostile. The enmity took a definite form under the emperor Domitian, in the closing years of the century. It had long been the custom in certain cities of the East to worship the emperor as a god on earth, and Domitian resolved, for political reasons, to make this Caesar-worship the official religion. For the people generally it was nothing but a harmless formality, which provided extra festivals and enabled them to manifest their loyalty; but to the Christians this usurpation by a human being of the honor due to God was revolting. They refused to take part in the stated ceremonies, and thereby exposed themselves to punishment as bad citizens. The danger was serious, but in the effort to confront it the church was strengthened and consolidated. It was purged of unworthy members who had joined it for the sake of worldly advantage and were only a source of weakness. It was compelled to forget all internal differences in the struggle with a common enemy. Above all, it was inspired with a new pride in Christianity as a heroic calling. Each believer was a soldier of Christ, and must be prepared, if need be, to sacrifice his life.

Two New Testament writings, very different in character, have come to us out of that time of persecution. The First Epistle of Peter is sent from Rome, which is compared to Babylon, the tyrannous city denounced by the prophets. That Peter himself wrote the letter is more than doubtful. His name appears only in the opening verse, and may have been inserted by a later editor, along with one or two touches at the end. The teaching of the Epistle is closely modelled on that of Paul, the opponent of Peter, and its language is an excellent Greek, which the Galilaean Apostle could not have acquired in his old age. If he was one of the victims

FIRST AGE OF CHRISTIANITY 171

of Nero's massacre he must have been dead for thirty years at the time when the Epistle was written. But whoever may have been its author it is one of the most beautiful of the New Testament writings, steeped from beginning to end in the genuine spirit of Christianity. Word has come to Rome that the churches of Asia Minor are suffering persecution, and the letter is written to comfort them and exhort them to faith and courage. They are reminded of all that they owe to Christ, and of the example of patience which he gave them. They are made to realize the greatness of their religion, and to feel that the one path of safety is to follow out its teaching more consistently. As we read this Epistle we can see that persecution has strengthened and purified the church. Its members have been drawn closer together by their common suffering. They have learned through their sacrifices to prize their faith and to understand more of its meaning.

The book of Revelation is likewise a summons to hope and patience in the face of calamity. Before the recovery of the Jewish apocalyptic writings this book was regarded as altogether mysterious, shadowing forth in dark symbols the secrets of the unseen world and the distant future. We can now see that it is only one example, by far the most splendid, of a once familiar type of literature. It does not deal with future events but with those of its own day, and most of its riddles can be spelt out from our knowledge of the history. The writer is one of the leaders of the Asian church, and has been exiled in the persecution to the lonely island of Patmos. From there he addresses his fellow Christians, especially those of seven churches to which he sends urgent messages, conveyed to him by the Spirit from the exalted Christ. Most of the book is occupied with prophecies of doom, but their purpose is to inspire hope and confidence. It was assumed in apocalyptic thought that immediately before the end there would be a time of awful crisis. The powers of evil would put forth their mightiest effort, and the present order would crumble into utter ruin, before the breaking in of the new age. In the agony which has now overtaken the church the writer sees the beginning of this darkest hour before the dawn. The faithful have to endure for just a little while longer, and Christ will appear and crown them with victory. For the author of Revelation Rome is the great enemy, the impious power which Satan has raised up to oppose the cause of God. Its wickedness has now reached its height in the blasphemous Caesar-worship. The approaching downfall of Rome is foretold in cryptic language and imagery, to which Christians alone would have the key. There had been a rumour widely current in the previous generation that the wicked emperor Nero had not died but had escaped to the East, and would presently return at the head of an avenging army. The author of Revelation gives a new turn to this popular belief. Nero has indeed died, but will rise again as the Antichrist—the devil's Messiah—to

FIRST AGE OF CHRISTIANITY 173

take part in the last conflict.[39] Terrible days are near but the end is certain. Rome will perish, Satan with all his powers will be overcome, the suffering church will emerge triumphant as the Bride of Christ. He will set up his Kingdom on earth with a new Jerusalem let down from heaven as its centre. His people will there reign with him for ever.

It is difficult to say how far the author intended his highly symbolic pictures to be understood in a literal sense. Probably he did believe that the world was approaching its final crisis, and that Rome, the persecuting city, was presently to suffer the vengeance of God. He little anticipated that Rome would one day be the capital of the church, that the social order which appeared so hopeless would be regenerated, that the cause of Christ would triumph not by a sudden miracle but by an effort sustained through long ages. But with all its strange imagery and old-world ideas the book has a permanent religious value. Not only does it give matchless poetical expression to the Christian hope of immortality, but it is inspired throughout by a magnificent spirit of faith, which was to justify itself far more wonderfully than the writer could foresee. In that hour of darkness when the church seemed utterly helpless under the iron heel of Rome, he declared that the cause of God was certain to triumph, whatever powers might be arrayed against it. Since Rome had challenged the church it was not the church but Rome that would

---
[39] Rev. xiii.

go down. At the time it must have seemed a madman's dream, more fantastic than any of the visions that now puzzle us in the book. Yet within three centuries the religion of that little persecuted sect had conquered the world. Rome itself, the haughty Babylon, drunk with the blood of saints, had become the city of the church.

CHAPTER VI

THE DEVELOPMENT OF NEW TESTAMENT THOUGHT

(I) THE NATURE OF THE DEVELOPMENT

The New Testament as we now possess it forms a single volume, which is accepted by all branches of the church as authoritative. From later interpretations of Christian belief we turn confidently to that which is set before us in the New Testament, forgetting too often that this one book is made up of a large number of writings which were produced at different times and in different places during a period of more than a century. Their authors were men of the most diverse training and temperament, and were sometimes in sharp conflict with one another. Not only so, but the century which gave us the New Testament was the youthful, formative period of our religion. All opinions and institutions were then fluid, and far-reaching changes were effected rapidly and almost unconsciously. The advance in Christian thinking was far greater within that one century than during the next fifteen hundred years.

It is only in our own time that we have learned to study the New Testament as a literature rather than as a single book. The chief effort of scholars formerly was to harmonize the various writings, and to make out that under different forms of expression they contained the same doctrines. This effort has now been abandoned. It is frankly recognized that there is no such thing as a uniform New Testament teaching. To be sure there are certain great beliefs which are fundamental with all the writers, and they share in the same general outlook and temper. Their thought, however widely they differ from each other, has a freshness and vitality which we do not find in the teachers who succeed them. The church was guided by a true instinct when it took these writings and set them by themselves as forming together a unique book, which was to be normative henceforth for Christian faith. But we can no longer read the New Testament as if it were the presentation of a single type of teaching. Within its brief compass it offers us a number of distinct types, which have all to be considered separately. In the century following the church settled down to those fixed beliefs which were finally embodied in the great creeds, and which reigned unquestioned almost to our own day. In the New Testament times only the broad principles of the new religion were accepted by all. Each outstanding teacher was at liberty to interpret them in his own way, in the light of his own Christian experience.

These types or phases which meet us in the New Testament may be thus classified. (1) The primitive beliefs, as they were held by the first Apostles at Jerusalem. (2) The theology of Paul. (3) The teaching of Paul's disciples—what is sometimes called the Deutero-Pauline teaching. (4) The type of thought which comes before us in the Epistle to the Hebrews. (5) The Johannine theology, represented by the Fourth Gospel and the Epistles of John. (6) The purely ethical Christianity reflected in the Epistle of James. (7) The apocalyptic Christianity, of which the great example is the book of Revelation. These phases of New Testament thought are all distinct from each other, and are known to us from their appearance in certain documents which happen to be preserved. From various allusions in the New Testament itself we can gather that alongside of them there were many other types of which we have no memorial. Paul tells us that at Corinth there were those who said, "I am of Apollos, I am of Cephas, I am of Christ."[1] What were the tenets of those forgotten parties? In the later New Testament books we hear much of "false teachers," working apparently within the church though proclaiming a strange gospel. The nature of this gospel we can only vaguely guess. Thus the Christianity of the age was marked by an endless variety. The message of Jesus was still new and unexplored, and earnest men everywhere were trying in their different ways to throw more light on it. In the New Testament we have the record of these many attempts to discover a little more of the hidden riches of the gospel.

Two facts have always to be remembered as we

[1] Cor. i. 12.

trace the history of New Testament thought. (1) The message proclaimed by Jesus legitimately offered itself to the later interpretations. It has sometimes been held that the original gospel was nothing but a nucleus which was gradually overlaid by a number of alien elements gathered in from many quarters. By this process of accretion, we are told, the simple message of Jesus was transformed into something different. But the truth is that with all its apparent simplicity the message was profound and many-sided. As soon as men began to reflect on it they found that it disclosed new and ever larger meanings. The first century was an age of intense intellectual activity. The great questions of life and religion were debated from many points of view—ethical, philosophical, social, mystical—and it was soon discovered that the Christian message could be understood in all of these aspects. When the New Testament writers seem to change it into something different they are seeking, as a rule, to bring out, under a new light, what it really contained. (2) It is customary to speak of the *development* of Christian thought in the New Testament, and this suggests that from the time of Jesus onward there was a continual unfolding of the gospel into something fuller and richer. In many respects, however, such an idea is quite misleading. It is certain that the disciples had understood Jesus very imperfectly and placed a narrow and often mistaken construction on his message. Paul, whom they regarded as an innovator, had a far deeper insight into its essential meaning; but his interpretation, too, was one-sided and inadequate. None of the later teachers attained to Paul's breadth of vision. After him, in spite of splendid exceptions like the writers of Hebrews and the Fourth Gospel, we can trace a gradual hardening and narrowing of Christian ideas. There was a development in the sense that the principles of Jesus were applied in ever new directions and on a wider scale. But the principles themselves were not broadened or deepened. Much that was most vital in the new religion was obscured or altogether lost as it travelled further from its beginnings.

(2) Primitive Christianity

Jesus had proclaimed the Kingdom of God and had taught the new righteousness by which men might enter it. Towards the close of his life he had revealed himself as the Messiah through whom the Kingdom would come. His disciples after his death took up his message, but inevitably it underwent certain changes which were destined to affect the whole later history. (1) The emphasis was now thrown on the Person of Jesus himself. He had dwelt almost wholly on the coming of the Kingdom, but the disciples were inspired by loyalty to himself. Now that he had been put to death as a false Messiah they felt that their supreme task was to vindicate him. Their faith in the Kingdom which he had proclaimed became indistinguishable from their faith in Jesus. (2) The tremendous events with which his life had closed could not but over-shadow everything that had gone before. He had died on the Cross and had risen again. It was impossible henceforth to think of his gospel apart from these amazing facts. All that he had said and done in his lifetime seemed to point forward to his death and to find explanation in the light of it. The message of the Cross came more and more to constitute the very substance of the gospel. (3) Assured that he was the Messiah and had now risen from the dead the disciples could no longer think of him merely as the Master whom they had known on earth. Whatever he had been he was now the exalted Lord, who was soon to come again in the clouds of heaven. Readers of the New Testament have often wondered that so little reference is made outside of the Gospels to the actual life of Jesus. Does it not appear as if his personal followers were callous and forgetful, or that the life they had witnessed had made little impression on them? But their silence is to be explained on just the opposite grounds. They had been so profoundly impressed by Jesus that they were convinced that he was still living, and that they did not need to dwell on his past career in pious reminiscence. Their whole thought was concentrated on what he was now, and on what he would be when he presently returned.

At the beginning there was no thought in the mind of the disciples that Jesus had been nothing less than the founder of a new religion. They took for granted that his work was only a stage in the history of Judaism, and that the Law and the sacred institutions still remained in force. Where they differed from other pious Jews was in their acceptance of Jesus of Nazareth as the promised Messiah. They claimed that this belief, so far from separating them from their old religion, marked them out as its true representatives. God had chosen Israel to be His people and had promised them a salvation which would be wrought at the appointed time by the coming Messiah. This hope had been central in the religion of Israel, and it had now been fulfilled in Jesus. Those who believed in him were therefore the true Israel. This apparently was the significance of the name, borrowed from the Old Testament, by which the Christian society called itself. Though it was only a small minority of the nation it was yet the "Ecclesia," the genuine community of God's chosen people.

The church began, then, as a sect within Judaism; but from the first it was distinguished, in two important respects, from other Jewish communities. (1) Its members were possessed with a consuming enthusiasm. They were convinced that the new age, of which Jesus had spoken, was on the point of dawning. He had died to bring in the Kingdom, and presently would return to complete his work. Those who believed in him would inherit the new age, and their mood was one of strained expectancy. They were "those who waited for the coming of the Lord." The watchword by which they recognized one another was "Maranatha" "The Lord is coming."[2] This mood expressed itself in the

---
[2] I Cor. xvi. 22.

belief that a supernatural power, the Spirit, was at work in the church. The presence of such a power seemed to be clearly attested by the wonderful capacities with which even the humblest of the believers were now endowed. They "spoke with tongues"—in a strange ecstatic utterance which seemed to be more than mortal language. They broke out into prophetic rhapsody. They showed a courage and self-denial, a spiritual insight and ardor of faith which they had not known before. All this could mean nothing else than that Jesus, now exalted, had sent that divine Spirit of which the prophets had spoken to guide and strengthen his people. (2) This enthusiasm went hand in hand with a practical obedience to the precepts of Jesus. Believing that he was the Messiah his disciples accepted his teaching as the true way of life. His sayings were handed down and collected, and formed a rule of conduct for the new community. By membership in it you were committed to the type of life which Jesus had taught and exemplified. You were a follower of "the Way."[3] From the outset this moral obedience was demanded, and it was this that ensured the future of the new faith. If it had been nothing but an apocalyptic excitement it would quickly have died out, when the hope of an immediate return of Christ had proved mistaken. As it was, the enthusiasm did not spend itself in empty emotion, but gave wings to the new endeavour towards a higher moral life.

[3] Ac. xix. 9, 23; ix. 2.

The religion of the early church thus centred in the belief that Jesus was the Messiah and would presently return in his true character to bring in the Kingdom. All thinking had for its object the proof of the Messianic claim. The life of Jesus was reviewed in the light of Old Testament prediction. It was shown that he was descended from David, that his works of healing were in line with the ancient anticipations, that his whole ministry had followed the course mapped out in prophecy for the Messiah. But there was one great difficulty which at first seemed insuperable. No indication was offered in Scripture that the Messiah was to die at the hands of his enemies. All the prophecies had assumed that his career was to be one of victory, and Jewish opponents were not slow to point out that the claim of Jesus made shipwreck on the fact of the Cross. The chief task of the disciples was to remove this stumbling-block. Christian theology may be said to have its root in the effort to explain the death of Christ.

One triumphant answer to all doubt lay ready to hand. Men had slain Jesus as a false Messiah, but God had vindicated his claim by raising him from the dead. It was not enough, however, to maintain in this way that the death had been a terrible mistake. The grand episode in which the life of Jesus had culminated could be no mere accident. Not in spite of his death but somehow by means of it he must have accomplished his Messianic work. In this effort to discover a supreme significance in the death of Christ the church took its stand on Isaiah's great prophecy of the Servant of God, who suffers and dies to atone for the sins of others (Isa. xlii., xlix., liii.). It can hardly be doubted that this mysterious figure is meant to personify Israel, or the righteous remnant of Israel, and in this sense the passages had previously been interpreted. But the church accepted this section of Isaiah as the central Messianic prophecy. The Old Testament itself had foreshadowed the death of Jesus and had attached a meaning to it which was henceforth normative for Christian thought. When Paul enumerates the elements of faith which he had received from the Apostles before him he puts this in the foremost place; "Christ died for our sins according to the Scripture."[4]

In that earliest Christianity, as reflected in the opening chapters of Acts and in stray references by Paul, we are not to look for any reasoned doctrines. The disciples were content with a few enthusiastic beliefs—that Jesus was the Messiah; that he was presently to return in glory and bring in the Kingdom; and that meanwhile he had endowed his people with the Spirit. These beliefs, which grew up spontaneously in the early days, continued to be fundamental to all later theology. In the course of the next century they assumed new and unexpected forms, but did not essentially change.

The church had hardly begun its mission when it drew numerous converts from the Hellenists or

[4] I Cor. xv. 3.

Greek-speaking Jews, who were resident in Jerusalem. They introduced an element which was destined in the end to transform the character of the whole movement. No Jews were more loyal to the old beliefs and customs than those of the Dispersion, but in their contact with the great Gentile world they had acquired new points of view—they had learned to employ ideas derived from the Greek thinkers for the interpretation of their own religion. With Stephen and his colleagues this more liberal spirit found its way into early Christianity. The author of Acts introduces a long chapter which he regards as the speech delivered by Stephen at his trial.[5] It has little relevance to the supposed circumstances, but all the more for this reason we may be confident that it is an early document, typical of the nature of Stephen's teaching. The drift of its argument seems to be twofold: (1) to prove that the church is representative of that true Israel which has never been more than a small portion of the nation; (2) to show that what God requires is a spiritual worship. Those visible institutions of which Judaism made so much were at best mere types and prophecies. "The Most High dwelleth not in temples made with hands," and the old religion has now attained through Christ to its loftier stage. This conception of the spiritual nature of worship had already been powerfully maintained by Philo, the great Jewish thinker of Alexandria. It was afterwards to find immortal utterance in the declaration of the Fourth Gos-

[5] Ac. vii.

pel—"God is Spirit, and those who worship Him must worship in spirit and truth."[6] In the teaching of Stephen we can trace it for the first time as one of the governing ideas of Christianity. The Hellenistic influence has already become a real factor in Christian thought.

This influence became increasingly powerful as the Gentile mission advanced. The gospel, which had sprung out of Judaism, was now carried into a world to which Jewish thought and belief were entirely foreign. Such terms as "the Messiah" and "the Kingdom of God" were familiar to the Jew, but to the Gentile they had to be explained. He could respond to the great religious ideas involved in them only when they were expressed in a manner congenial to his own mode of thought. The missionaries set themselves to this task of explaining the gospel, and they did so the more readily as they were themselves Hellenists and more deeply affected than they knew by the Gentile influences around them. In this process of interpretation the message inevitably underwent a change and lost something of its original meaning. At the same time the new forms of thought were in many ways more adequate than the old. There were elements in the Christian message—and these among the most vital—which could never have come to their own within the narrow confines of Jewish tradition.

This process of Hellenizing the gospel has often been regarded as wholly due to Paul. He has been

---
[6] Jn. iv. 24.

accused of wilfully distorting the message as Jesus had taught it, with the result that all the centuries since have missed the true meaning of Christianity. But it is well to remember that the Hellenizing process was inevitable. It had begun before Paul. It was advanced, during his own lifetime, by many teachers who worked quite independently of him. There can be little doubt that a great deal of what we call Paulinism was not Pauline but Hellenistic. Paul is the one Apostle whose writings have come down to us and he therefore receives the sole blame or credit for everything he taught. But he was only one of many missionaries who all drew, as he did, on those Hellenistic ideas which were in the very atmosphere of the time.

Of these missionaries, however, he was by far the greatest, and was peculiarly fitted for his task of interpreting Christianity to the Gentiles. He was himself a Jew of the Dispersion, trained in the Rabbinical schools and yet acquainted from childhood with the Gentile ideas. He possessed in a rare degree the sympathetic mind which could throw itself without effort into sentiments and points of view which were different from his own. Above all, he was a man of supreme religious genius, with a deep insight into the inner meaning of Jesus' message. While expressing it in new forms, often, it might appear, foreign to its nature, he was able in a wonderful way to preserve it and to bring out, more clearly than ever, the truth at the heart of it.

(3) THE THEOLOGY OF PAUL

Paul was the first Christian theologian. The Apostles before him had proclaimed the gospel; Paul set himself to understand and explain it. His explanation cannot, however, be reduced to any coherent system. His surviving Epistles were all intended for definite occasions, and were thrown out, as a rule, in the heat of controversy. Their statements are always fragmentary and sometimes contradictory. Paul, too, had not the type of mind which carefully builds up a system. He was emphatically a man of genius, passionately interested in the truth that occupied him for the moment and concerning himself little with its precise bearing on other truths. He thought not by rules of logic but by flashes of intuition, and believed that his gospel had come to him by direct revelation of the Spirit.[7] All the later theological systems have been based on him, but he himself had none.

Paul is thus often inconsistent in his thinking, but he is always real. Even when he works with ideas which we now feel to be arbitrary and obsolete he is trying to account to himself for some genuine religious experience. It is this which gives his writings their perennial vitality. We are always sure, as we read them, that he is dealing with spiritual facts, which repeat themselves in the life of every Christian. His explanations may not sat-

---
[7] Cf. Gal. i. 11, 12.

FIRST AGE OF CHRISTIANITY 189

isfy us but no other thinker has so vividly realized the facts.

His theology was rooted, then, in his own experience. He was conscious that through his knowledge of Christ a marvelous change had been wrought in him. What was its nature, and how had it come about? He can describe the change in one word—deliverance or "redemption"—but this only brings him to the threshold of his problem. What is the bondage from which Christ has delivered us? No doubt it is a moral bondage, and Paul affirms, as Jesus had done, that men are enslaved to their own evil wills, and can only find freedom when they are inwardly renewed. But how had they fallen into this subjection to sin? Paul tries to find an answer to this question. His object is to prove that Christ has delivered from sin by overcoming the conditions that make for sin.

It is here that we encounter the chief difficulties in Paul's thinking. In his analysis of the ultimate causes of sin there is much that now appears strange and fantastic. Sometimes he connects man's sinfulness with the fall of the first man, Adam, which has involved the whole race in moral ruin.[8] Sometimes he traces everything back to demonic agencies which have conspired against us and against which we are helpless.[9] Most often he discovers the true cause of sin in the *flesh*. Man in his inner personality is a child of God, and perceives that the

---
[8] I Cor. xv. 22; Rom. v. 12.
[9] Eph. vi. 12.

will of God is the law of his being. But this higher nature is involved in a lower one which drags him down, and frustrates all his efforts toward better things.[10] There can be no deliverance until the power of the flesh is destroyed.

At this point we recognize the Hellenistic influence. Centuries before Paul the Greek thinkers had reflected on the problem of man's misery, and had arrived at the conviction that there is something amiss with the very basis of our existence. The body in which we find ourselves is a tomb or prison. Matter and spirit are in conflict with each other, and in this material world we can never know true freedom. For Greek thought, therefore— and its conclusions had now been reinforced by Eastern pessimism—evil was bound up with the very constitution of man's being. Not his will only but his nature was at fault. Paul takes up this idea in his attempt to discover the meaning of the work of Christ. Man is a spiritual being who yet is carnal, "sold under sin," and in order to free him from sin Christ had to destroy the power of the flesh.

Paul's thought is complicated by the importance which he attaches to the Law. He was a Jew, brought up in the belief that religion was inseparable from the Law, and even as a Christian he could not entirely rid himself of his old sentiment. He was engaged, too, for most of his life, in controversy with the Jewish party in the church,

---
[10] Rom. vii. 18 ff.

which insisted that the Law as well as faith was necessary to salvation. We cannot wonder that he interprets the new method of salvation in the light of its contrast with the Law. This contrast was indeed a real and far-reaching one. Judaism sought to impose God's will on man by means of a rigid code, outwardly prescribed, while Christianity aimed at an inward change, which would make all formal rules unnecessary. Paul's criticism of the Law has a permanent value, as Luther discovered when he was called on once again to combat a mechanical type of religion. Yet the legal controversy which bulks so largely in Paul's Epistles belongs to the circumference of his teaching. It was forced on him by historical conditions, and had little to do with his deeper reflection on the gospel.

He himself declares this in so many words when he describes the Law as nothing but an interlude in the history of God's dealings with men.[11] That the Law was divinely given he cannot, in the face of the Old Testament, deny; and he has therefore to find some place for it in the purpose of God. But he maintains that its place was never more than a subordinate one. Before men could understand their need, and respond to God's offer of deliverance they had to realize their sinfulness. It was brought home to them by the Law, which plainly set before them a moral ideal to which they could never attain. Not only so, but the Law created the sense of guilt, and thereby changed sin into an intolerable burden. By its stern prohibitions, too,

[11] Gal. iii. 15 ff.; Rom. vi. 20.

192 FIRST AGE OF CHRISTIANITY

it worked on the propensity of human nature to do the things that are forbidden.[12] Paul is thus led to his strange conclusion that the purpose of the Law was not to mitigate sin but to increase it. Before God could interpose for man's redemption sin had to reach its maximum, just as an ulcer has to come to a head before the physician can offer relief. The Law was thus an intermediate stage in the discipline of mankind. Paul compares it to the guardian whose business it was to check and control the schoolboy until he was fit for liberty.[13] The Law has now accomplished its temporary work and has been done away.

It was the legal controversy, however, which enabled Paul to define with perfect clearness the great principle which he henceforth placed at the centre of his gospel. From the outset the church had laid emphasis on *faith*. No one could enter the brotherhood unless he believed in Jesus as the promised Messiah, and professed this belief in the solemn rite of baptism. As yet there was no suspicion that this faith was incompatible with the Law, to which all Jewish Christians conformed as a matter of course. But with the progress of the Gentile mission the question became acute—"must all who believed in Jesus submit to the Jewish Law as well?" Paul took his stand on the position that faith alone was sufficient. He maintained this position at the Council of Jerusalem, and later, when his work was attacked by the Judaists, he asserted

---
[12] Rom. vii. 7,8.
[13] Gal. iii. 24.

it still more vehemently. Faith, he declared, was the living principle of Christianity and was radically opposed to the Law. Men must choose either the one or the other.[14]

In this assertion of faith as the one thing needful, Paul was led to reflect more deeply on its meaning. What was involved in the act of belief in Christ? To answer this question he had to ask himself the inner purpose of Christ's work, which was summed up for him in the death of Christ. On the Cross Christ had died for our sins. The Cross, therefore, stood for a supreme act of grace on the part of God. Men had been trying to satisfy God by painful yet futile obedience to the Law; now they had been freely forgiven through that great act of Christ. It followed that the Cross was the revelation of the true character of God. He had hitherto been conceived as a task-master, rewarding men strictly according to what they could earn in his exacting service. But this, it was now apparent, was to misunderstand the nature of God. He does not bargain and pay, but freely gives. He is the God of grace, and in Christ we have the assurance of this boundless generosity of God.

Since this is the nature of God, what must be our attitude towards Him? It must no longer be one of fear and calculation, as under the old legal system. If God is the great Giver, all that he requires on our part is the willingness to receive. This, for Paul, is the meaning of faith. If we believe that

[14] Gal. ii. 16. Cf. Rom. iii. iv.

Christ was God's messenger and that he died for our sins, we open our hearts, in that very act of belief, to receive from God. Faith is that receptivity on our part which answers to the divine grace. It is Christ who evokes this faith, and Paul can thus speak of faith in Christ, or more definitely in the Cross of Christ. But faith in Christ is at the same time faith in God, for in Christ we have the supreme manifestation of the gracious purpose of God. From the beginning God has been revealing Himself as the Giver, but men have doubted Him and have feared to commit themselves to his mercy. But in the Cross He has offered us his "unspeakable gift,"[15] and we can no longer mistake his will towards us. Inasmuch as "He spared not his own Son but gave him up for us all," we know Him as the God of all grace.[16] Our attitude to Him can be no other than that of faith.

Over against the Jewish theory of salvation through the Law Paul therefore sets his doctrine of Justification by Faith. The ultimate meaning of this doctrine is simply that God bestows his forgiveness freely, but Paul cannot state his belief in these plain terms, as Jesus does in the parable of the Prodigal Son. Not only must he answer the defenders of the Law, but he himself is still haunted by the Jewish idea that God can only show favour to the righteous. If sinners are accepted it can only be because they have somehow become righteous, and are so placed on a new footing before God.

---

[15] II Cor. ix. 15.
[16] Rom. viii. 32.

He maintains, therefore, that the effect of faith in Christ is to secure a Justification or acquittal. Men are sinful and so liable to the condemnation which God pronounces on sinners, but on the ground of their faith God considers them righteous. He confers on them a righteousness which they could not win for themselves, and on this ground admits them to his favour.[17]

This doctrine of Justification by Faith exposed Paul in his lifetime to grave criticism, as it has often done since. It was objected that men were encouraged by it "to do evil that good might come."[18] The Law, whatever might be its shortcomings, had insisted on certain moral demands, apart from which all religion was vain. Paul had declared that men might trust implicitly in the grace of God. The more plentiful their sins the more they would illustrate the greatness of the divine grace. To be sure Paul had spoken of a Justification obtained through faith, but it did not effect a real righteousness. Faith at best resulted in a sort of fiction by which men were accounted righteous while they were still in their sins. There was force, as Paul himself acknowledged, in these criticisms, and his answer to them is not entirely satisfying. Yet when we look not so much to the answer itself as to its underlying purport, we can accept it as valid. He holds that in the act of faith the will is set in a new direction. Sinful desires and impulses lose their control; the love of God takes possession of

[17] Rom. i. 17; iii. 21-26.
[18] Rom. iii. 8; vi. 1.

a man's heart, so that henceforth his one aim is to serve God. As hitherto he rendered himself a willing servant to evil passions, so now he becomes obedient to God. Faith in Christ marks the beginning of a new life, in which the whole nature is transformed.

At this point we come to the deeper and more characteristic side of Paul's teaching. He thinks of the redemption through Christ not merely in a negative way as a deliverance from sin, but positively, as the entrance on a new and higher life. How is this life made possible? What does it consist in? As he tries to answer these questions Paul ceases to avail himself of Jewish categories, and falls back on others, borrowed from Hellenistic thought.

The religions of the time all turned on the need for some higher and more enduring *life*. A conviction had grown up that human misery was ultimately due to the fact that we are creatures of earth, endowed with an inferior kind of life. Was it not possible to change this life into one of higher quality, resembling that of celestial beings? We should then be free from debasing passions and from the power of fate and death. The so-called "mystery-religions" now coming in from Egypt and the East, professed to satisfy this craving, and here was the secret of their wide appeal. They had all grown out of a primitive nature-worship which celebrated the revival of vegetation after the blight of winter. The primitive mind had construed this annual miracle in the form of a myth, which was

FIRST AGE OF CHRISTIANITY

broadly the same in all the religions. A youthful divinity had been destroyed by a cruel enemy but had been restored to life. As spring came round a festival was held to commemorate his death and deliverance, and in course of time it came to bear a mystical significance. By enacting in a sort of drama the experience of the god the worshippers sought to repeat it in themselves. In symbolic fashion they died with the god in order to pass with him into the immortal life on which he had now entered. From much of the language of Paul it can hardly be doubted that he was acquainted, in some manner, with these mystery religions. This is not surprising, for their annual celebrations were a familiar spectacle in all the great cities. The ideas on which they rested had passed into the religious thought of the time, and were familiar to the readers for whom he wrote his Epistles. With that keen intellectual sympathy which enabled him to gather in suggestions from every quarter he seized on their main conception in order to express a meaning which he saw in the gospel. Christ had died and risen again as the representative of men. His people were to enter into union with him. Sharing in his death they were to rise with him into newness of life.

It is easy to make too much of this affinity between Paul and the mystery cults. Some modern writers have inferred from it that in the course of the Gentile mission Christianity lost its original character and was construed on the pattern of those Oriental religions which had gained currency in the empire. Jesus was assimilated to the mythical "Lords" of the cults; his gospel was transformed into a matter of sacraments and mystical theosophy. The truth is that the central mystery idea of dying and rising with the Redeemer is peculiar to Paul, and that it constitutes only an aspect of his thought. For the most part he works with ideas derived from the Old Testament and contemporary Judaism, or from the beliefs of the primitive church. Most of all, we have to reckon with his endeavour to find adequate expression for his own Christian experience. He was conscious of a change effected in him by Christ, which none of the traditional ideas could fully account for. Christ must have been more than the Messiah of the Jewish hope; his work had secured a redemption that would avail not only in the future Judgment, but here and now. In his endeavour to set forth these deeper meanings which he saw in the gospel Paul was attracted to the strange conceptions embodied in the Pagan cults. They would impress him the more because they sprang from the belief in a death and resurrection. Might it not be that the heathen had darkly apprehended a great truth, although they had perverted it and applied it to the service of false divinities? In the gospel it had found its true fulfilment. Christ had died and passed through death into a higher life, thereby ensuring a new life for his followers. With his Hellenistic training he was naturally disposed to many of the ideas involved in the cults. He shared in the belief that evil is inherent in earthly and material conditions. He

FIRST AGE OF CHRISTIANITY 199

thought of man as surrounded by malign, semi-personal powers from which he could be delivered only by divine assistance. It was not unnatural that he should be influenced, consciously or not, by the mystery religions.

This influence, then, while it must not be exaggerated, cannot be ignored. There can be little doubt that from this side certain elements of the utmost consequence entered into Christian thinking. (1) A new significance was attached to the Person of Christ. For the primitive disciples he had been the Messiah—a heavenly being who was higher in dignity than the angels but who yet shared their nature, not that of the supreme God. Now he was conceived as in some real sense divine. The name "Lord" which had hitherto been only a vague title of reverence, was understood in something of the same sense that it bore in the mystery cults. Christ was "Lord" inasmuch as he was a divinity to whom worship could be offered, and through whom men could enter into direct fellowship with God. (2) The two peculiar rites which the church had practised from the first were now construed as *sacraments*. Baptism had originally been nothing more than "the baptism of repentance for remission of sins," the rite by which the convert declared his break with the old life and assured himself of divine forgiveness. The Lord's Supper was the solemn pledge that Christ would presently return, and that his people would share with him in his Kingdom. The Christian ordinances were now assimilated to those of the contemporary religions. In all of these there were sacred rites, sometimes curiously resembling baptism and the Supper, which were supposed to confer a supernatural grace on the worshipper. By means of such rites he entered into direct relation to the god. The experience of the god was repeated in him, and his nature was thereby changed into something higher. From the time of Paul onward a like virtue was attributed to the Christian ordinances They ceased to be merely symbolic rites and became in the full sense sacraments. (3) A mystical strain, which was foreign to its original character, now found entrance into Christianity. For the Hebrew mind God was the heavenly King, separated by an infinite gulf from the world which He had created. Man's attitude to Him could only be one of awe and utter obedience. No angel, and much less a man on earth, could participate in the life of God. Such a union with God, however, was the whole object of the mystery religions. At the heart of them lay the conviction that God was present in his creation, and that the soul of man had proceeded from God and was ultimately one with Him. The purpose of all their rites and discipline was to induce a state of ecstasy in which the worshipper should escape from himself and share, if only for a moment, in the divine being. Christian piety, under the foreign influence, now took this mystical direction. It was not enough to believe in Christ and to grow like him by obedience to his commandments. True faith in Christ had its outcome in union with Christ. He himself took possession of the believer and enabled him henceforth to live the divine life. The deepest motive of Paul's religion finds expression in his constantly repeated formula "in Christ." He was assured that in some manner he had become one with Christ, and that this was the secret of the new life into which he had entered. "It is no longer I that live, but Christ liveth in me."[19]

In his effort to explain the new life which arises through faith in Christ, Paul thus avails himself of ideas which were offered him by Hellenistic religion. He thinks of Christ as a divine being who had died on behalf of men and had risen again. By his death he had done battle with man's enemies and had overcome them. Above all he had vanquished the principle of the flesh—the lower, earthly nature to which man had hitherto been enslaved, and which was the seat of sin. In faith and baptism we assimilate ourselves to the victorious Christ. Dying with him we die to the old sinful life and partake in that new life on which he entered by his Resurrection. Henceforth though we continue in the body we are inwardly united with Christ and rise with him into newness of life.[20]

Paul expresses his conception in another way by means of his doctrine of the Spirit. From the primitive church he inherited the belief in a supernatural power which manifested itself in Christian worship, and in those new energies of which Chris-

---
[19] Gal. ii. 20.
[20] Rom. vi. 3-7.

tians were now capable. Hitherto the Spirit was associated solely with those strange gifts, but Paul conceived of it as a power which controlled the whole life when a man had put his faith in Christ. Those who were once "carnal," at the mercy of sin, became "spiritual," so that all their thoughts and motives and desires were set in a new direction.[21] But while the Spirit reveals itself in a new moral energy, and most of all in love, which is its supreme gift,[22] it is something more than a power which renews the will. It changes the constitution of a man's being. Proceeding from God it makes our nature similar to the divine nature, and the moral change which it effects is only a consequence of this more radical change. Paul's conception of immortality connects itself with this doctrine of the Spirit. He looks forward to a future life which is guaranteed by the fact of Christ's Resurrection, but he believes that this life after death will be only the outcome and consummation of that new life which has already begun. By possession of the Spirit our nature is mysteriously changed and has part in the immortal life. As yet this higher life is hidden and potential.[23] The believers, like other men, continue in their earthly bodies and are subject to bodily weakness and decay. But after death the body which now is will be replaced by a "spiritual body," fitted to be the vesture and instrument

---

[21] Rom. viii. 1-16.
[22] I Cor. xiii.
[23] Col. iii. 3.

of a purely spiritual life.[24] Paul sometimes speaks of it as a "body of glory," and seems to imagine it as woven out of an ethereal substance akin to light.[25] He was confident that he himself had seen Christ, on the way to Damascus, clothed in this "spiritual body."

Paul's doctrine of the Spirit continually merges in his doctrine of union with Christ. Often indeed he speaks of the Spirit as if it were identical with the indwelling Christ. He sometimes turns in the same sentence from the work which Christ effects in us to that which is accomplished by the Spirit. In a sense the conception of the Spirit, although it occupies such a large place in his thinking, was superfluous for Paul. He took it over from the primitive church as an essential element in Christian belief, and gave it a far grander and richer meaning. But all that it signified to him was contained already in his conception of the mystical union with Christ. With all his effort he cannot prevent the two doctrines from merging at every point in one another.

Paul's teaching on the new life is highly mystical and speculative, but it is related in the closest manner with his ethical ideas. His Epistles invariably close with a chapter of practical counsels, often in abrupt contrast to the lofty theological chapters which have gone before. But when we look more closely we discover that the homely moral precepts

---
[24] I Cor. xv. 35-44.
[25] Phil. iii. 21.

have grown out of the theology. From his exposition of the nature and origin of the new life he proceeds to show how this life will manifest itself in actual Christian conduct. It is in his ethical teaching that we most clearly perceive the essential agreement of Paul with Jesus. Here and there he falls back on Jewish maxims, or avails himself of suggestions from the Stoic philosophy. But the profoundly Christian character of his ethic is unmistakable. The three virtues which he accounts highest—faith, hope, and love—are those which he had learned from Jesus. The manifold directions which he gives to his converts are all conceived in the spirit of the Sermon on the Mount. Nowhere in his morality can we detect anything that is at variance with the principles laid down in the Gospels. It is true that he seldom quotes a literal saying of Jesus, but this was doubtless due to his resolve "not to know Christ after the flesh." [26] Conceiving of Jesus as the living and present Lord he was not content to repeat his precepts in their familiar historical form. He sought to lay hold of their inner purport and so apply them to the new conditions which he encountered in the great cities of the Gentile world. But while the ethic of Paul is fully in harmony with that of Jesus there is one significant difference, due to his Hellenistic mode of thought. Jesus puts the whole emphasis on the renewal of the will. Men are children of God but have allowed their will to become per-

---

[26] II Cor. v. 16.

verted and must bring it into unison again with the will of God. Paul thinks of the new will as unattainable without a change of nature. Men are fleshly, and therefore incapable of any good, but by the operation of the Spirit the power of the flesh is cancelled. Evil desires and impulses are destroyed, and the higher moral life grows up of its own accord as the "fruit of the Spirit."[27] By placing his ethic on this metaphysical basis Paul involves himself in constant difficulties. Logically he is forced to the position that Christians, in whom the sinful instincts of the flesh have disappeared, are no longer capable of sin; yet the fact is all too patent that they are still subject to temptation and often fall. Thus he is compelled to make a distinction between the actual and the ideal condition of the Christian man. His exhortation takes the form, "you have been set free from sin by Christ; strive to become in very deed what you ideally are."

It is not difficult to point out the limitations of Paul's thought. He works with the Jewish and Hellenistic ideas of his own time, and much of his argument has now lost its force. He had come to Christianity through a peculiar experience, and with a mind and temperament which were in every way exceptional. Even in his own lifetime his gospel was far too individual to find acceptance with the church at large, and perhaps there has

[27] Gal. v. 22.

never been a Christian who could be called in a full sense a follower of Paul. Yet our debt to him is incalculable. He was the first to attempt a reasoned account of the gospel, and all theology since has been built on the foundation which he laid. Although his teaching as a whole has never been accepted he threw out a multitude of ideas, many of which are still as living and fruitful as ever. With a matchless insight he pierced to the essential meaning of the Christian message. While the earlier disciples were still concerned with adjusting the gospel to the paramount claims of the Law, Paul perceived clearly that Jesus had given a new religion, based on new principles. He defined once for all these vital principles—faith, liberty, moral renewal, loyalty to Christ in whom God had revealed Himself, and reliance on the divine power which has entered the world through him. Paul's greatness consists in the certainty with which he apprehends and expresses these central truths of the gospel. The manner in which he expresses them is different from that of Jesus. He seems at times to change their character in his effort to state them in the categories of Gentile thought. But his message is ultimately the same as that which meets us in the Gospels, and this inner identity is all the more impressive because the form and language are so different. We are made to feel that the truth of our religion is not dependent on any set mode of presentation. It may clothe itself from time to time in new forms while still remaining the same.

(4) The Pauline School

The letters of Paul himself are accompanied by certain others which are strongly marked by his influence, and may be assigned to his disciples. (Ephesians, I and II Timothy, Titus, and I Peter).

The most remarkable of these writings is the Epistle to the Ephesians, which is still regarded by many scholars as the work of Paul himself.[28] Whoever wrote it had entered deeply into Paul's spirit, and reproduces much that is most characteristic in his teaching. The main interest of the Epistle, however, is in one idea which is suggested by Paul but never fully developed—the idea of the church. As the writer looks back on the work of Christ he finds its chief significance in the creation of the church. He thinks of the church as the larger incarnation of Christ, as the mystical body of which Christ is the Head.[29] Within this brotherhood all differences have been done away. Jews and Greeks have been brought together, and the oppositions and misunderstandings which have hitherto sundered the human family have disappeared.[30] The writer is thus led to a profound theory of the divine purpose as revealed in the church. In this community of Christ's people on earth he sees the beginning of a work of reconciliation which will finally embrace the whole universe As yet there is strife and confusion everywhere, but God has planned to bring all things at last into

---
[28] See Chap. v., sect. 6.
[29] Eph. ii. 22, 23.
[30] Eph. ii. 11 ff.

perfect harmony. In Christ he has revealed His ultimate purpose, and through Christ He will complete the work which He had in mind at the Creation. The church which Christ has brought into being, and in which all discordant elements have been reconciled, is the first fruits of the great consummation.[31] Since this is the purpose of the church, a plea is made for unity within the church itself. All rivalries and oppositions and dissident teachings are to cease, so that the church may exemplify within itself the peace which will at last extend through it to the whole world. The Epistle to the Ephesians is one of the noblest of the New Testament writings, and historically it is of the first importance, as illustrating the value which the idea of the church was assuming for Christian thought. At the time when it was written the church was an obscure society, made up of perhaps a hundred scattered groups of believers. But already it was confident of a mighty future. It had begun to conceive of itself as the mystical body of Christ, through which he would fulfil God's final purpose with His whole universe.

The *Pastoral Epistles* (I and II Timothy and Titus) also bear witness to the growing sense of the value of the church, but they are concerned more with its outward organization than with its inward idea. That Paul wrote these Epistles as we now have them is hardly possible. In their style and thought they bear little resemblance to the other Pauline Epistles; they place the Apostle

---
[31] Eph. iii. 9 ff.

in circumstances which cannot be fitted in with the known story of his life; they are written in view of ecclesiastical conditions which did not come into being until after his death. The writer is an earnest man with lofty ethical ideals, which he sometimes expresses in powerful language, but he shows little insight into the deeper meaning of Christianity. There is a touch of the commonplace in his thought which we cannot associate with Paul, least of all with that crowning period of his life from which these Epistles profess to date. They probably contain a few genuine fragments, which can be identified by various tests. These had fallen into the hands of a disciple who expands them into letters which he believes that Paul might have written if he had been confronted with the problems which had since arisen. There are three main interests in the letters. (1) They insist on the simple moral obligations, which were in danger of being neglected, now that the church was absorbed in high speculative questions. (2) They proclaim the necessity of right belief. The false teachings which had invaded the church in Paul's lifetime had now grown into dangerous heresies. Christian ideas were thrown into strange combination with the wildest extravagances of Paganism, with the result that they were utterly distorted. In view of this Gnostic peril the writer demands a return to "sound doctrine."[82] He wishes to have the essential teachings of Christianity so defined and established as to form a barrier against the in-

[82] I Tim. i. 10; II Tim. i. 13; iv. 3; Tit. i. 9; ii. 1.

roads of all foreign belief. (3) As the main protection against this danger he desires to strengthen the church as an institution. Its order must be made definite and its discipline enforced, and for this purpose its officers must be invested with proper authority. Paul is made to address Timothy and Titus, two of his most prominent assistants, giving them directions which they are to follow in their missionary work. He authorizes them to act boldly in the suppression of abuses, and calls on all members of the church to submit themselves to these duly appointed officers.

(5) THE ALEXANDRIAN INFLUENCE

Toward the end of Paul's life a new impulse, fraught with far-reaching consequences, began to act on Christian thinking. It came from Alexandria, the second city of the empire and the chief centre of its culture. The successors of Ptolemy, to whom Egypt had fallen in the division of Alexander's conquests, had been munificent patrons of art and letters. They had drawn to their capital the literary and philosophical leaders of the Greek world, and around the splendid library which they founded there had grown up what we should now call a university. Owing to its proximity to Palestine Alexandria was largely settled by Jews, and the keener minds among them had thrown themselves eagerly into the intellectual life of the city. They had developed a new type of Judaism, orthodox in practice but bold and liberal in thought, which aimed at combining the religion of the Old

Testament with the Greek philosophical conceptions. The chief exponent of this Alexandrian Judaism was Philo (B.C. 20-A.D. 50), a large number of whose works have been preserved. Philo is chiefly memorable for his influence on Christian theology, but on his own merits he is entitled to rank among the great thinkers of the ancient world. His aim was to interpret the Jewish beliefs in the light of Greek speculation, and this he did by the method of allegory. He assumed that since the Old Testament was given by the Holy Spirit its literal statements were all to be understood in a spiritual sense. Where it dealt with historical incidents it was describing, in a parable, experiences of the soul. Where it spoke of men or places it signified moral qualities. The ordinances it laid down had reference always to some inward condition, not merely to an outward act. Philo applies this method in quite arbitrary fashion to the books of the Law, and has little difficulty in discovering that Moses had anticipated all the profoundest ideas of the Greek thinkers.

He takes his departure from the familiar Greek conception of Reason as the governing principle of the world. In the Stoic philosophy it was maintained that Reason pervaded all things like a fiery essence, and that the soul of man is a spark from this universal reason. Stoicism, in its original form, put this pervading reason in the place of God. Philo, with his Jewish instinct, could not accept this philosophical pantheism. He held that the reason which made and sustains the world is the reason of God, and is subordinate to Him. God in Himself is solitary and transcendent, but His reason goes forth from Him like the radiance from the sun, and accomplishes his will. The Greek term "Logos" denotes both reason and spoken word, and Philo took advantage of this double meaning. We hear constantly in the Old Testament of God acting through his word of power, in the creation and government of the world and in the revelations imparted to holy men. So Philo thinks of a Logos which is at once the word of God and his reason. It is one with God and yet separable from Him—a second divine principle through which the sovereign God enters into relation to His world. The soul of man is related to this divine Logos, and by union with it can lift itself to God. In varied imagery Philo describes the Logos as the high-priest, the shepherd of souls, the cupbearer who pours out the divine life, the mediator between God and man. He conceives of worship, though it must express itself in outward forms, as inward and mystical. It consists in the effort of the soul to lay hold of the divine Logos and so rise out of the earthly material sphere into communion with God.

It is not difficult to see how this philosophy lent itself to Christian purposes. From the beginning the church had been striving after a conception of Christ which should answer more fully to the value he possessed for growing Christian experience. He had first been regarded as the Messiah, but this idea, even in its loftiest forms, was felt

FIRST AGE OF CHRISTIANITY 213

to be inadequate. The Messiah of Jewish tradition was at most an angelic being, higher than all angels but still separated from God by the whole gulf that must lie between the creature and the Creator. There could be no assurance that through such a Messiah the believer could apprehend God. Paul had thought of Christ as the Lord, but this idea, with its suggestion of a mere secondary divinity, was also inadequate. Philo offered the conception of a being who was other than God and who yet, in the fullest sense, partook of His nature. This interpretation of the worth of Christ alone seemed to satisfy the demands of Christian piety. How the doctrine found entrance into the church we do not know; perhaps through Apollos and men like him who had been trained in the Alexandrian school. Paul himself in his later days, as we may gather from the Epistle to the Colossians,[33] was feeling his way toward the Logos theology, though it never took a primary place in his thinking. In the generation after him it came more and more to dominate the whole Christian attitude toward the Person of Christ.

(6) THE EPISTLE TO THE HEBREWS

The new influence is conspicuous in the so-called Epistle to the Hebrews. This remarkable writing, which bears all the marks of a spoken discourse though it closes with epistolary notes and greetings, may be assigned to a date about 85 A.D. It was probably addressed to the church at Rome, or

---
[33] Col. i. 15-17.

rather to one of the numerous groups into which that great church was divided. Many attempts have been made to determine its authorship, but we know too little of the church leaders of that later period to arrive at any conclusion. The title "to the Hebrews" was attached to it at an early time, in view of its many allusions to the Old Testament and to Jewish ritual. Many scholars, even in our own day, hold the opinion that it was intended for Jewish Christians who were in danger of falling back into their old religion; but this is almost certainly a mistaken view. At the close of the first century the distinction of Jews and Gentiles in the church had disappeared. The writer, moreover, hardly touches on the Law, which in this age, after the temple had fallen, was the one basis of Jewish religion. It is now coming to be recognized that the Epistle was not addressed to "Hebrews" but to Christians generally, who by reason of persecution or mere lapse of time were growing listless in their faith. The writer seeks to restore them to ardor and constancy. He declares that in Christianity they possess the absolute religion. It enables them to pass beyond all shadows and symbols and set their faith on the ultimate realities. It gives them access, amidst all the world's changes, to God Himself. In order to prove this surpassing worth of Christianity the writer contrasts it with that levitical system by which, in former times, men made their approach to God. He tries to show that in Christ we have the true Highpriest, and that the ancient ordinances were only types and anticipations of his work. In place of those animal sacrifices which were offered year by year on the day of Atonement and at most could only secure a ritual purity, Christ has made the one all-sufficient sacrifice of himself, and by means of it has purged our sins.[34] As the high-priest passed through the veil of the tabernacle and stood for a brief interval before God on behalf of the people, so Christ passed through the heavens and now sits forever at God's right hand. There he intercedes for us continually. He has brought us into a relation to God which can never be interrupted.[35]

In his presentation of this argument the writer makes use of ideas which have come to him through the Alexandrian philosophy. He never directly applies the term "Logos" to Christ, and from this we may infer that there was still a prejudice against it. None the less his conception of Christ is determined by the Logos idea. The opening verses of the Epistle, which tell of the Son through whom God created all things and who was "the effulgence of his glory and the impress of his substance," are couched in the very language of Philo. The Philonic influence is still more marked in the idea which underlies the whole argument of the Epistle and which comes to light in the ever-repeated contrast of earthly and heavenly, seen and unseen, temporal and eternal. It is assumed that over against the visible world there is an unseen world which is the true one. By faith we can set our

---
[34] Heb. vii.
[35] Heb. ii. 11 ff.

hearts on this higher world amidst the illusions of time, and so give meaning and reality to our lives. The work of Christ, as this writer conceives it, was to bring us into living relation to those eternal things.

In its essential thought, therefore, the Epistle goes back to the Platonic teaching as interpreted by Philo. But this philosophical strain is curiously blended with another, derived from the very earliest type of Christianity. Like the primitive disciples the author thinks of the church as the consummation of the history of Israel; he looks forward to the speedy return of Jesus as Messiah; he works with the ideas of Jewish apocalyptic and conceives of the ministry of Christ as enacted in a literal sanctuary, which is the heavenly counterpart of the holy place on earth. It is this mingling of primitive ideas with those of Greek speculation which makes the Epistle in many respects so difficult. Some of its glowing passages, and above all the glorious eleventh chapter in praise of Faith, are among the chief treasures of Christian literature, but the argument as a whole is obscure, and often impresses us as artificial and trivial. But when we penetrate its meaning the Epistle is throughout a noble presentation of a great theme. The writer is not a mystical thinker like Paul, and does not draw like him out of an intense personal experience. He shows little understanding of some aspects of the gospel which we rightly regard as primary. But he gives splendid utterance to his own conception of the meaning of Christianity.

Through Christ we have the knowledge of a higher world; we can lay hold of the realities which cannot be shaken; we can possess in the fullest measure that faith which has been the secret of the heroic life in all ages. By means of this Epistle a new element of inestimable worth was brought into our religion.

(7) THE GOSPEL AND EPISTLES OF JOHN

The Alexandrian influence which is clearly traceable in the Epistle to the Hebrews, is still more pronounced in the Fourth Gospel and the kindred Epistles of John. One of the chief problems of the New Testament is concerned with the authorship of these writings, and unless some new and unexpected evidence comes to light it will never be solved. According to the church tradition they were the work of John the son of Zebedee, one of the three foremost disciples of Jesus. This tradition might seem to be confirmed by the closing chapter of John, which declares that the Gospel was written by the beloved disciple who has appeared several times in the course of the story. It is clear, however, by its own testimony, that this chapter was added to the Gospel by its earliest editors, and when we examine it more closely we can see that they were themselves doubtful of the authorship, and threw out a guarded conjecture. That the Gospel was the direct work of the Apostle John is hardly possible. All the evidence, external and internal, appears to show that it was written in the first decade of the second century, when John can no longer have been alive. It is based on the Synoptic Gospels, of which an actual eye-witness would have felt himself independent. It presents a picture of Jesus not as he appeared to his actual disciples but as men thought of him long afterwards, when a Christian theology had been fully formed. If the Apostle John had anything to do with the Gospel it must have been indirectly, as the master who is ultimately responsible for its teaching. According to one view which has found acceptance with many scholars the author was not the Apostle but another John, who is known to early Christian Fathers as "John the Elder," and who was a prominent figure in the Asian church about the turn of the century. Our book of Revelation was not improbably the work of this Elder, for the author expressly says that his name was John, and addresses himself to the churches of Asia. No two books, however, could be so different as Revelation and the Fourth Gospel. Not only in thought and language but in their whole religious attitude they are manifestly the products of two different minds. If John the Elder was the author of Revelation he cannot have written the Gospel.

There can be little doubt that whoever wrote the Fourth Gospel was also the author of the First Epistle of John and the two brief Epistles which accompany it. They are cast in the same mould of language, and are at the same time too original to be mere imitations. Indeed the First Epistle is in its own way just as wonderful as the Gospel, and serves to supplement and illuminate its teaching.

FIRST AGE OF CHRISTIANITY 219

This Epistle was called forth by the heretical movement which had attracted large numbers of Christians who prided themselves on their superior philosophical culture. Jesus, as the new teachers represented him, was a divine being who had only appeared to wear a human body and live a human life. His work had consisted in the revelation of a secret doctrine, which only the more gifted natures were capable of understanding. In virtue of their higher knowledge they had obtained the true life, and might hold themselves aloof from the moral obligations which were binding on ordinary Christians. The First Epistle of John is written to a church which had suffered from the inroad of these strange doctrines. Some of its members had left it in order to form a select intellectual group by themselves.[36] Those who remained were troubled by the suspicion that the gospel as taught by the older missionaries was out of date. Men of culture and enlightenment would not have grown so zealous for the new doctrines unless they represented a higher truth. The writer of the Epistle sets himself to answer these misgivings. He declares that the effort to change the gospel into something deeper and more mysterious had impoverished it, and charges his readers to hold fast to "the old commandment which they had from the beginning," admitting no new beliefs which are not in full accord with it.[37] He offers them certain plain, practical tests whereby they may know the gen-

[36] I Jn. ii. 19.
[37] I Jn. ii. 7, 8.

uineness of their Christianity, and insists above all on the test of love. If they have learned to love one another they may be sure that they have truly understood the gospel of Christ. If they fancy themselves to be possessed of a profound wisdom and are thus tempted to hold aloof from their brethren, their wisdom must be false. Only as we grow in love towards our fellowmen do we advance in the true knowledge of God in Christ.[88]

The First Epistle was probably written later than the Gospel, for it sometimes alludes in a passing word to ideas which are developed in the larger work and are hardly intelligible without it. Yet the Epistle may be regarded as the key to the Gospel. It enables us to place the evangelist in his surroundings and to understand the practical interests with which he wrote. Often he has been described as a daring innovator. He undertook, we are told, to assert the divine character of Jesus at the expense of the actual history. Possessed with his idea that Christ was no other than the eternal Word he reviewed the earthly life and transformed it into a kind of allegory. But the real purpose of the Gospel must be conceived as just the opposite. At the time when it was written the chief danger to the church was from the Gnostic emphasis on the divinity of Jesus, and the evangelist wishes to assert the reality of the earthly life. That is why he throws his work into the form of a Gospel. From the misty speculations of the age he falls back on the actual record, and shows that it must

[88] I Jn. iii. 14 ff.

FIRST AGE OF CHRISTIANITY 221

be read as historical fact. To construe it as mere myth or allegory is to miss its whole religious value. Jesus was the Saviour of men because he was himself a real man. He brought the divine life into our earthly sphere and so enabled us to make it our own. "The Word was *made flesh* and dwelt among us."[39]

This great statement, however—the thesis on which the Gospel is founded—has another side. That which was made flesh and so came within our human compass was *the Word*. We are never allowed to forget that the Teacher who worked in Galilee or Jerusalem for three short years was the Son of God, and that all his words and actions had therefore a divine significance. The Gospel is not intended to be literal history. While it presents the facts of the life of Jesus, and insists that they were facts, it is chiefly concerned with their inward meaning. The life is viewed throughout under two aspects—that which it bore to those who actually witnessed it, and that which it still has for the believing soul. Jesus gave bread to the hungry multitude, and thereby revealed himself as the bread of life for mankind. He raised Lazarus from the dead, in order to show that for all who accept him he is the resurrection and the life.[40] He healed a blind man, and we are meant to realize, as we read the incident, that he was the Light of the world.[41] All that he was as he moved visibly

---
[39] Jn. i. 14.
[40] Jn. vi., xi.
[41] Jn. ix.

among men was only the suggestion of what he is still in the spiritual realm. Thus the earthly life of Jesus, as the evangelist tries to present it, was the prelude and foreshadowing of his larger life in the time to come. Earlier Christian thought had centred on the hope that Jesus who had departed into heaven would one day return. John boldly declares that this return has taken place already. The death of Jesus was nothing but his release from those conditions of space and time which limited him while he lived on earth. Henceforth he dwells with men as an invisible presence, entering into their very hearts and revealing himself more fully and intimately than he was able to do to his first disciples.[42] Thus the Gospel is at once a narrative of the life on earth and an adumbration of the invisible life that was to be. It culminates in the discourse to the disciples at the Last Supper, in which Jesus speaks explicitly of the fellowship which his people would have with him hereafter. All that had gone before had been only the preparation for that inner communion in which he would reveal himself to those who had not seen and yet had believed.

The work of Christ, as John conceives it, is summed up in the two words, Light and Life. On the one hand he was the Light, the full revelation of God. "He that hath seen me hath seen the Father."[43] The Synoptic Gospels also describe Jesus as the Revealer. He knew the will of God

---
[42] Jn. xvi. 22 ff.
[43] Jn. xiv. 9.

and disclosed it in his teaching, so that men in their moral action might be children of their Father in heaven. There is little revelation of this kind in the Fourth Gospel. Jesus does not speak of the moral nature of God and His will to men, but of his own relation to Him as the Son in whom we know the Father. It is in this sense that he brings the revelation of God. Through him the divine nature has come within the range of our knowledge. Hitherto we could only surmise that beyond all things visible there was the unchanging God, but now we can apprehend Him as a reality. And as he was the Light, Christ was the Life. Here again the primary reference is not to that moral goodness which in the Synoptic teaching constitutes true life. John conceives rather of a divine life which is different in kind from that of men—self-existent, immortal, and exempt from all human frailty. This life which God possesses dwelt also in Christ, and the great end of his coming was to impart it to men. As creatures of flesh they are debarred from the true life.[44] Thy are subject to earthly accident and passion and ignorance, and by no effort of their own can they rise out of this condition, which is best described as one of "death." But in Christ the divine life entered into this lower world. Men can so unite themselves with Christ that a new life-principle takes possession of them. They undergo a mysterious change which is nothing less than a new birth.[45] They become of

---
[44] Jn. iii. 5, 6.
[45] Jn. iii. 3.

spiritual nature instead of mortal men. For John, therefore, the true resurrection takes place in that moment, marked by the act of baptism, in which a man unites himself by faith with Christ. He then "passes out of death into life,"[46] out of the natural, earthly condition into the higher one. Physical death can make no difference to the man who is thus inwardly changed. He has entered already on his immortal state of being.

In these Johannine ideas we perceive the influence of Paul, who likewise thought of Christian faith as resulting in a new life, different in kind from that into which we are born. But the teaching of the Fourth Gospel is determined by another influence, of which we find little or no trace in Paul. The evangelist sets out from the conviction that Christ was no other than the Logos—the eternal Word which Philo had defined as a second divine principle, the creative and revealing energy of God. What to Philo was an abstraction becomes for the evangelist a personal being. The Logos had existed from the beginning with God, and had finally assumed the nature of man in Jesus Christ. It was for this reason that Christ was the Light and the Life. He brought the revelation of God because he was himself of the same nature as God. He communicated the higher life because he possessed it in himself, as the Logos, the Son who was one in essence with the Father.[47] The Logos idea is explicitly set forth only in the Prologue of the Gos-

---
[46] Jn. v. 24.
[47] Jn. i. 4.

pel (i. 1-18), but we are meant to read the whole narrative that follows in the light of these opening verses. Jesus, while he consorted with men, was the Word become flesh, and everything he said and did had therefore a divine value. After his death he resumed his higher state of being and is now an all-pervading presence endowed with sovereign power, although he still remains one with the Friend and Master whom we knew on earth.

The full adoption of the Logos doctrine marked a great advance in Christian thought. By means of it an alliance was made possible between the new religion and the general intellectual movement of the age. The Logos idea was the outcome of centuries of Greek thinking, and by accepting it the church made itself heir not only to the Law and the Prophets but to all the higher speculation of the ancient world. It may further be said that the new conception gave a truer and more satisfying expression to Christian piety than any that had preceded it. When he thought of Christ as the divine Word the believer could feel that his religion had an absolute value, that in Christ he was brought into immediate relation to God Himself. At the same time the Logos doctrine entailed a grave departure from the original message of Christianity. It caused all emphasis to be thrown on metaphysical questions instead of on the practical issues of the Christian life. Jesus himself had conceived of God, not as absolute Being, but as the Father whom we can love and trust. He had declared that the great need of men was a change of will, which would produce a moral likeness to God. He had stood forth as the representative of God inasmuch as he impressed on men the goodness and holiness and redeeming will of God. With the adoption of the Logos doctrine God was defined in terms of being; the work of Christ was made to consist in the mysterious process whereby human nature is transmuted into divine. We cannot but feel that for centuries afterwards the mind of the church was set in a wrong direction. The paramount questions presented to it were not "How may we best serve God?" "How may we find release from evil motives and desires?" "How may we carry the spirit of Jesus into our personal lives and into the life of the world?" They were rather "What is the precise relation of Christ to God?" "What is the mysterious grace which he imparts, and how is it imparted?" Religion became primarily a matter of the intellect and not of the mind and heart.

The fourth evangelist, however, could not foresee these consequences. With him the religious interest is always dominant, and he makes use of the highest philosophy of his time in order to affirm it in what seems to him the fullest and grandest way. He was assured that in Jesus the mind of God was manifested. He was conscious of a new life which had come to him through the knowledge of Jesus. He recognized that the power of Jesus was working still, even more mightily than when he had visibly lived with men. All this he tried to express by his doctrine of the Word which had been with God from the beginning and by which

FIRST AGE OF CHRISTIANITY 227

the divine life imparted itself. The permanent message of the Gospel is little affected by the limitations of the Logos philosophy through which it is conveyed. It is no mere accident that after the opening chapter the evangelist ceases to insist on the doctrine with which he set out. He is so overpowered by the beauty and grandeur of the actual life of Jesus that he half forgets to think of him as the Word become flesh. Millions who have read the Gospel have never suspected that it has a theological purpose. To press its doctrinal teaching unduly is indeed to do it a grave injustice. The writer is not so much a theologian as a man of profound religious nature, alive to the inmost meanings of Jesus' life and teaching. Not without reason did the earliest editors identify him with that beloved disciple of whom he wrote.

The Gospel itself suggests to us that we must not be bound by any elements of its teaching that belong merely to the thought of its own age. One of its governing ideas is that of the Spirit, which Jesus bestowed on his followers when he himself departed. The work of the Spirit is to "lead men into all truth."[48] Jesus had proclaimed his message in a given land and time, and under the necessary limitations imposed on him by his place in history. The Spirit was to take up the message after his death and set it forth in new language. "He will take the things that are mine and will show them unto you." The evangelist knew himself to possess this living Spirit, and his aim is to reinterpret

---
[48] Jn. xvi. 12-14. Cf. xiv. 25, 26; xv. 26.

the gospel to the new generation which had arisen in the Greek world seventy or eighty years after Jesus had departed. It was the same gospel but had now to be thrown into new forms, corresponding to the thought of the later time. But the evangelist never meant that his interpretation should be final. He believed that the Spirit which had inspired him would work continually in the church, unfolding the message of Christ, and presenting it in new forms to each new age.

(8) Popular Christianity

Our knowledge of the early church is derived from the New Testament, but the impression it leaves on us is in some ways a mistaken one. We assume that the writers of these books were representative of the church at large, and wonder at the rapid development of such a profound theology out of the primitive Christian teaching. It is too often forgotten that Paul and the author of Hebrews and the fourth evangelist were great original thinkers, and that the church as a whole lagged far behind them. In every age the vast mass of Christians have troubled themselves little with high speculations. They have held to a theology of their own, which has often differed widely from that of the few rarely gifted minds. It was not otherwise in the first century, and for proof of this we have only to turn to the New Testament itself. Along with the writings of the great teachers it has also preserved for us several others, which evidently reflect the more popular type of thought. They seem

FIRST AGE OF CHRISTIANITY 229

at first sight out of place, and it has sometimes appeared strange that they should have found their way into the New Testament. But they are probably more typical of the religious ideas of the time than the writings which we would now rank far above them. One of these documents of the popular religion is the book of Revelation.[49] It was written, only a few years before, in that same region of Ephesus which gave us the Fourth Gospel, but its character is altogether different. The author of the book, with all his splendid faith in the future of the church, knows nothing of that spiritual interpretation of its message which we have in the Gospel. For him Christianity is still an apocalyptic hope, as it had been for the first disciples. He believes that Christ will presently return in visible glory and set up a Kingdom which will endure for a thousand years and have its centre in a new Jerusalem. In the events of his time he traces the beginnings of the great crisis which will soon overtake the world. He thinks of Christ not as an indwelling presence but as the heavenly champion of the church, rewarding its martyrs and destroying its enemies. Much in the book is consciously symbolical, but the apocalyptic conceptions of the unseen world are accepted as substantially true. God is a Sovereign enthroned in heaven, who effects his purposes through a host of attendant angels. A Judgment will be held in which all men will have their destinies assigned to them. The

---
[49] See Chap. v., sect. 7.

wicked will be cast into a fathomless abyss while the just will rest from their labours in Paradise.

The apocalyptic ideas are likewise taken for granted in the short Epistle of Jude and the so-called Second Epistle of Peter, into which it was expanded about the middle of the second century. Attacking the false teachers who had endangered the faith and morality of the church, the author of Jude looks forward to a judgment soon to come when the Lord will descend from heaven and punish all evil-doers. Not only does the Epistle move in an atmosphere of apocalyptic thought but it quotes directly from the book of Enoch, one of the best-known apocalyptic writings.[50] For the author of the Epistle—and he was doubtless typical of a large body of opinion within the church—the Jewish apocalypses had all the authority of inspired Scripture.

Another tendency, however, was equally characteristic of the popular Christianity of the time. The church had set out not only with an apocalyptic hope but with a new morality, based on the precepts of Jesus. This ethical side of the message had always been emphasized, and was now pressed by many Christian teachers to the exclusion of all else. With Jesus himself morality was inseparable from religion. It was his chief criticism of the Law that it made right living a purely legal matter—obedience to a rule which had been laid down. He insisted that it must flow directly out of the reli-

---
[50] Jas. xiv.

FIRST AGE OF CHRISTIANITY 231

gious impulse, and that otherwise it has no worth. Men are to enter into a new relation of love and trust toward God, so that their will may be inwardly conformed to His will. For Paul, too, moral action has its spring in religion. The hidden life of the Spirit, according to his favorite metaphor, produces its visible fruits in every kind of right conduct. He contrasts this spontaneous morality of the Spirit with the "works" done mechanically in obedience to the Law

But it was only the higher minds in the church who understood this new Christian conception of the moral life. Jews and Gentiles alike had been accustomed to think of morality as depending on stated rules, and when they became Christian they still required to have their duties definitely marked out for them. Too often when an effort was made to realize Paul's idea of a morality of the Spirit it was construed wrongly. Christian freedom was interpreted as the right to dispense with all ethical sanctions and follow the caprices of one's own will. Even in Paul's lifetime his gospel was sometimes perverted into a charter for self-indulgence; and with the spread of Gnostic ideas the danger became still more pronounced. The Gnostics, pushing the doctrine of Paul to what seemed its logical conclusion, declared that the God of the Old Testament was different from the Father of Jesus, —an inferior and tyrannical God. It was the duty, therefore, of the Christian to throw off the moral law which the Jewish God had imposed on men before they had learned that he was not supreme. It is easy to understand how the sounder conscience of the church was revolted by such teaching, and the reaction against Gnosticism brought with it a distrust of the Pauline doctrine of freedom. Before the end of the century we have signs of a growing belief that Christianity was a "new law." Jesus was a greater Moses, who had destroyed the old law in order to replace it with another, far superior to it but of the same order. The precepts he had enounced were detached from their vital connection with religious principles and were set forth by themselves as the moral code now binding on all Christians. This moralism is represented in the New Testament by the Epistle of James. Ascribed as it is to James the Lord's brother, the leader of the primitive church at Jerusalem, the Epistle has often been regarded as the earliest New Testament writing; but it may be confidently set down as one of the latest. The ascription to James has nothing to support it but the title at the beginning, and this was prefixed most likely by an editor who guessed that this Epistle, with its rigorous morality, must have been written by no other than James the Apostle, the unbending champion of the Law. This guess is almost certainly mistaken. The writer, so far from maintaining the claims of the Jewish Law belongs to a time when the very meaning of Paul's controversy with the Law had been forgotten. In a passage which seems to be directed against the Pauline teaching he assumes that the Law denounced in Galatians is the moral law, while

FIRST AGE OF CHRISTIANITY 233

faith is nothing but a bare assent to the Christian beliefs.[51] Such a reading of Paul's position is as far as possible from the truth.

The Epistle is pervaded by a lofty ethical spirit. The writer insists on perfect sincerity in word and deed, and will have nothing to do with a religion that consists merely in fine sentiment. The one test of a man's faith is his practical behaviour. A striking feature of the Epistle is its sympathy with the poor, as against the well-to-do converts who were now finding their way into the church, and to whom many were inclined to pay an undue deference.[52] The readers are exhorted to treat all men as brethren and to practice charity, humility, patience, and submission to the will of God. But while he thus exalts the Christian virtues the writer makes little or nothing of the Christian motive. For this reason his work has sometimes been regarded as in substance a Jewish tract, which he has taken over for the purpose of Christian edification and garnished with a few Christian phrases. This is certainly to do him an injustice. His moral ideals are those of the Sermon on the Mount. Everywhere he shows himself steeped in its spirit, and occasionally he makes use of its actual language. But this Christian morality is taken as something by itself. The author is impressed by its rightness and beauty but has never pondered on that new idea of God and our relation to Him

[51] Jas. ii. 14–26.
[52] Jas. ii. 1 ff.

out of which it grows. A similar detachment can be observed in other writings of the later period which have not been included in the New Testament. In that age of speculation there was a grave danger of turning Christianity wholly into a theological system, and the ethical reaction was needful and salutary. Yet we cannot but feel that the earlier teaching has become warped and impoverished. In the Gospels all the elements of the religious life have their due place, and this harmony is still preserved in the Epistles of Paul. The later teachers apprehend the message one-sidedly. They make it purely intellectual or mystical or ethical, and so fail to present it in its full significance. Our religion has suffered ever since from this overemphasis on some one aspect of its message to the neglect of all the others. If we would know something of its comprehensiveness we have still to go back to the beginning.

As we survey the development of Christian thought in the later New Testament period we can see that it was governed by three main factors. (1) There was a growing realization, in the light of Christian experience, of the far-reaching implications of the message of Jesus. As it was taken up by men who differed widely in their thoughts and interests each of them discovered some new meaning in it and interpreted it in his own way. Paul, John, the writer to the Hebrews, James, the seer of Revelation, might almost appear to stand for different religions, which have only a few ideas and phrases in common. Yet they are all dealing with the same gospel, and read nothing into it which it did not in some measure contain. The difference is only in the minds of the thinkers, who respond to separate aspects of the message. (2) Christianity had become a Gentile instead of a purely Jewish religion. This change entailed a statement of the gospel in new terms. The ideas of Jesus were interpreted in the light not only of Hebrew prophecy but of Greek philosophy and Oriental mysticism. It cannot be denied that their original purport was thus in many ways modified and even distorted. Yet the new categories in some respects gave a truer expression to the mind of Jesus. There was a breadth in his thought which was not Jewish, and we often feel, as we read the Gospels, that he is seeking to break through the limits which were imposed on him by the ideas he had inherited. Through the adoption of Greek instead of Jewish conceptions some of the vital meanings of the gospel were liberated for the first time. The teaching of Jesus seems to undergo a transformation but in reality has come to its own. (3) The church was building itself up into a world-wide institution. This outward expansion cannot be separated from the inward growth. As we follow the course of Christian history in the times since we can see that historical changes have always reacted on theological progress, and this was never so apparent as in the first century. At the beginning each community stood by itself, each teacher was free to arrive at his own understanding of the message. In this atmosphere of liberty the mind of the church was able to develop with wonderful rapidity in every direction. The first century stands out to this day as the great creative period in Christian thought. Almost all the theologies which have since been elaborated by a long succession of thinkers had their origin in that age. But with the expansion of the church this early freedom was no longer possible. It was apparent that unless the many individual groups could unite themselves in one great society the Christian movement would presently dissolve in utter confusion.

To secure the uniformity which was the necessary condition of further progress each community gave up something of its freedom. On all its members the church imposed a common type of worship, a common form of government. Most of all it insisted on unity of belief as the necessary basis of a united society. It was not till a later time that all within the church were required to assent to a formal creed, but in the New Testament itself we can trace the gradual approach to this demand. At the outset it was enough to make the general confession "Jesus is Lord,"[53] but after the death of Paul the meaning of this confession was more and more carefully defined. The progress of the "false teachings" had warned the church that faith could no longer be entrusted to the free guid-

---

[53] Rom. x. 9; I Cor. xii. 3; Phil. ii. 11.

FIRST AGE OF CHRISTIANITY 237

ance of the Spirit. If the gospel was to be transmitted in its purity there must be one authoritative form of belief.

Historically this fixing of Christian thought was necessary. Without an accepted creed there could have been no united church, and the great task of winning the world to Christianity could never have been accomplished. But the uniformity was not secured without a grievous loss. As we pass from the New Testament to even the greatest teachers of the following centuries we feel that the living impulse has died down. Christian thinkers are no longer explorers in a marvellous country, always discovering some truth in the gospel which had hitherto been unknown. Their course is mapped out for them beforehand. They are afraid to look and examine with their own eyes. The New Testament comes to us out of a time when the Christian mind was still unfettered. It is written by men who stood close to the life of Jesus, and on whom it had made its first overwhelming impression. They are conscious that it has a divine significance, which they strive to explain in the light of their own experience, the world's need, and the highest thinking of their age. Too often the New Testament has been treasured as the final and unchangeable statement of all Christian truth. Sincere and pious men have been persecuted because they ventured to differ, in some particular, from Paul and John. But those great interpreters of Christ would have been the first to acknowledge that they "had not yet apprehended." They were only seekers, and what they sought to bequeath to us was not some finished scheme of doctrine but their own spirit of tireless seeking. Realizing through them the depth and grandeur of our religion we can try, as they did, to learn more of its inexhaustible meaning.

INDEX

A

Access to God 214.
Acts, book of 109.
Adam 189.
Adonis 40.
Alexander 15.
Alexandria 122, 210 ff.
Annas 80.
Antichrist 136, 172.
Antioch 110, 127, 130.
Antiochus 16.
Apocalyptic 19, 90, 230.
Apollos 137.
Aquila and Priscilla 135, 137, 139.
Arabia 126.
Aramaic 50.
Archelaus 23.
Asmonaeans 16, 22.
Assyria 11, 12.
Athens 134.
Attis 40.
Augustus 20, 32, 38.

B

Babylon 11, 12, 34.
Baptism 118.
Barnabas 126, 132.
Beginning of the church 113 ff.
Beloved disciple 217.
Bethany 79, 80.
Bishops 163.
Brethren 119, 164.
Brotherly love 164.
Burial of Jesus 84 f.

C

Caesarea 149.
Caesarea Philippi 74.
Caesar-worship 43, 169, 172.
Caiaphas 81.
Capernaum 68.
Catholic church 169.
Census 24.
Christians, name of 122.
Church, doctrine of the 207 f., 235.
Church, origin of the 113 f.
Cilicia 123, 133.
Colossians, Ep. to 152, 213.
Conversion of Paul 123 ff.
Corinth 134.
Corinthians, 1st Ep. to 141 f.
Corinthians, 2nd Ep. to 143 f.
Council of Jerusalem 126, 192.
Creed, formation of 236.
Cross, message of 107, 180, 193.
Crucifixion 83 f.
Cyprus 127.
Cyrus 14.

D

Damascus 122, 124.
Daniel 19, 105.
David 12, 59.
Death of Christ 107.
Demons 70.
Destruction of Jerusalem 160.
Deutero-Paulinism 177, 207 f.
Development 178.

INDEX

Disciples 68, 85.
Dispersion 23, 185.
Domitian 169.

E

Ecclesia 118, 181.
Egypt 11, 34.
Ephesians, Ep. to 154 f., 207 f.
Ephesus 137.
Epistles of John 218 f.
Epistles of Paul 112, 188.
Essenes 29.
Ethical teaching of Jesus 98 ff.
Ethical teaching of Paul 204 ff.

F

Faith 192 ff.
False teaching 177, 209, 236.
Fatherhood of God 95.
Felix 150.
Festus 151.
Flesh 189, 201.
Fourth Gospel 49, 90, 138, 185, 218 ff.

G

Galatia 140.
Galatians, Ep. to 140 ff.
Galilee 24.
Gentile influence 162, 186.
Gentile mission 128.
Gethsemane 80.
Gnosticism 153, 158, 165 f., 220, 231.
Gospels 45 ff.
Government of church 162.
Grace 193.
Greek culture 15, 33.

H

Hebrews, Ep. to 177, 213 ff.
Hebrews, Gospel of 49.
Hellenistic influence 186, 190.

Hellenists 119, 129, 184.
Heresy 165, 219.
Herod Agrippa 129.
Herod Antipas 23, 66, 72.
Herod the Great 21 f., 59.
Immortality 17, 142, 202, 224.

I

Isaiah 184.

J

James (brother of Jesus) 129, 131.
James (brother of John) 130.
James, Ep. of 177, 232 f.
Jericho 75.
Jesus, Life of 58 ff.
Jesus, Teaching of 89 ff.
Johannine Problem 218.
John, Gospel and Epistles of 217 ff.
John the Baptist 46, 62, 74, 100.
John the Elder 218.
Jordan 64, 75.
Joseph of Arimathaea 84.
Josephus 46.
Judas 24.
Judas Iscariot 78, 80, 114.
Jude, Ep. of 230.
Judgment 92.
Justification 194.

K

Kingdom of God 62, 91, 101, 179.
Koran 25.

L

Laodicaea 155.
Last Supper 79, 115, 118, 143, 199.

INDEX

Law 14, 17, 30, 117, 130, 190, 232.
Life 196 f., 203, 233.
Light, Christ as 221.
Logos 211 f., 215, 224.
Lord, Christ as 199.
Lord's Prayer 93.
Luke 54, 109.
Luke, Gospel of 54 f.
Luther 141, 191.

M

Maccabees 16.
Malta 151.
Maranatha 181.
Mark, Gospel of 52, 86.
Mark, John 56, 128, 132.
Matthew, Gospel of 54 f.
Matthias 114.
Messiah 73, 102 ff., 183, 213.
Miracles 69.
Moralism 231 f.
Moses 12.
Mystery Religions 41, 196 f.
Mysticism 200.

N

Nazareth 61.
Nero 150, 160, 172.
New Birth 223.
New Law 232.
New Testament, formation of 168.

O

Obedience 96.
Official ministry 167.
Onesimus 152.
Organisation of church 163.
Oriental religions 40 f.
Orthodoxy 167.

P

Paganism 35.
Palestine 11 f.
Passover 79.
Pastoral Epistles 156, 208 f.
Paul, career of 123 ff.
Paul, theology of 188 ff.
Pauline school 207 ff.
Pentecost 115.
Persia 14.
Person of Christ 199.
Peter 56, 67, 115, 131.
Peter, 1st Ep. of 170 f.
Peter, 2nd Ep. of 230.
Pharisees 20 f., 71.
Philemon, Ep. to 153.
Philip 23.
Philip (evangelist) 120.
Philippi 133.
Philippians, Ep. to 155 f.
Philo 185, 211 ff.
Pilate 82.
Pliny 38.
Pompey 20.
Popular Christianity 228 ff.
Primitive teaching 179 ff.
Psalms 14.

Q

Q (symbol) 53 f.

R

Redemption 189.
Religious associations 36.
Remnant 118.
Resurrection 86 ff., 114, 142, 183, 201.
Return of Christ 222.
Revelation, book of 136, 171 f., 177, 229 ff.
Ritual 96, 214.

Roman empire 31 ff.
Roman religion 42.
Romans, Ep. to 146 ff.
Rome 21, 32, 122, 172.

S

Sacraments 200.
Sadducees 26 f.
Samaria 14.
Sanhedrin 28, 81.
Scribes 17, 26.
Seneca 38.
Serapis 40.
Sermon on Mount 98, 142, 233.
Servant of the Lord 184.
Silas 132.
Slavery 36 f., 153.
Solomon 13.
Son of man 105 f.
Spain 156.
Speaking with tongues 116, 182.
Spirit 116, 138, 164, 168, 182, 201 f., 227 f.
Spiritual body 202.
Stephen 120 f., 124, 185.
Stoicism 39, 204.
Synagogue 25 f.
Synoptic Gospels 50 ff.

T

Tacitus 47, 150.
Talmud 26.
Tarsus 123, 126.
Temple 12, 14, 60.
Temptation 65.
Thessalonians, Epp. to 135 ff.
Thessalonica 134.
Timothy 133, 135.
Titus 128, 143.
Trial of Jesus 80 ff.
Trial of Paul 156.
Types of NT teaching 176.

U

Uniformity 236.
Union with Christ 197, 200, 203, 223.
Unity of church 208.

V

Vatican hill 160.
Virgil 33.
Virgin birth 60.

W

Way, the 182.
Wesley 45.
Will of God 94 ff.
Women, ministry of 164.
Word, Christ as the 220.
Worship 162.

Z

Zadok 17.
Zoroaster 17.

www.ingramcontent.com/pod-product-compliance
Lightning Source LLC
Chambersburg PA
CBHW062017220426
43662CB00010B/1369